Inside Strategy:
Value Creation from within Your Organization

Shawn M. Galloway & Terry L. Mathis

For our parents

Thank you for your love, guidance, coaching and example, which helped us develop successful life strategies. For this, we are forever grateful.

Contents

Who is the customer? • what customers value • a constant question • forgetting • the urge to merge

CHAPTER 6: Vision

What is the vision? • Look both ways • performance-improving vision • becoming reality • be specific

CHAPTER 7: Rationale

What is the rationale? • making sense • the right questions • cultural acceptability • the significant few • cause and correlation • sell-by date

CHAPTER 8: Story

What's the story? • sticky ideas • emotional connections • simplicity • better results

CHAPTER 9: Boundaries

What's the scope? • beachheads • setting expectations • correcting course • transformational thinking

CHAPTER 10: Snipers or support?

What supports or conflicts with your ability to succeed? • buy-in • culture and habit • listening • dangers of copying • emotional reality

CHAPTER 11: Digging for data

What data-driven priorities would be of strategic value? • iterative process • deciding • signal and noise • lead, lag, and transform • new discoveries • interpreting • see what happens • relevancy

CHAPTER 12: Choosing

Which initiatives will best support your objectives? • quick wins • right speed • being wrong • the collective mind • decision defaults • consequences • options • thinking value

How will you create alignment? • connections • constant communication • one point of focus • tactical trouble • the messenger • support • making it easy • productive memes • checklist • keeping score

Tactical training • strategic education • hidden value • the framework • customers • vision • rationale • story boundaries • culture • data • choice • alignment • transforming

thinking the most are often the very people who ignore it. They spend all their time ricocheting from one emergency to another.

We're all familiar with the concept of return on investment, but what about return on attention? Priorities result from decisions. "No time for strategy" is a poor decision. Attention needs to be reallocated to thinking ahead. When short-term behaviors are misaligned with long-term vision, you're continually surprised by events. And some of these can be painful, if not outright dangerous.

Not paying attention to strategy is expensive. Each year organizations waste millions of dollars in time, resources, and effort. In our consulting practice we continue to see confusion: misunderstanding of strategy, real problems not addressed, misdirected effort, lack of personnel alignment, directionless short-term fixes, forgettable training, over-complexity, poor communication, cookie-cutter programs in place of strategic thinking, muddled motivation, poor incentives, not understanding what an existing organizational culture will tolerate or accept, misinterpretation of data, and attention to results without a clear understanding of how they came about. And these are just a few of the unproductive situations we encounter in our work.

But most of all we see a lack of focus on generating and measuring **ongoing contribution to value** throughout the organization. And, as you've probably guessed, contribution to value is the central theme of this book.

Strategic thinking can create value at just about every level of organizations. Today, managers and line-workers have increasing discretionary effort. They need a reason to guide and believe in what they choose to do. The best you can hope for with an alienated workforce is grudging compliance. No organization can afford disaffected workers. But influence hearts and minds, and hands and feet will follow. People need to be involved in decisions that affect them because projects tend to fail at the beginning, not at the end. Get the thinking right and implementation becomes relevant, easier, faster, and often cheaper.

Inside Strategy is not a recipe book. There are no sure-fire tips that will suit every situation, because you and your organization are unique. Instead we offer you a series of structured questions in Part II aimed at ongoing value creation. You can think of this as a checklist. This book is not so much what to do, but how to think about what to do. We wrote this book to stimulate your own thinking.

Finding your way

We've divided the book into three parts. Part I, Foundations, is an overview of important concepts: strategy, questioning, beliefs, and value. Part II, Framework, is a set of ten strategic performance-improving questions. Part III, Living Strategy, is how to sustain continual performance improvement.

Inside strategy's goal is first to understand and define effective strategy, then to focus it inside the company. The purpose is to improve performance and uncover previously hidden value from the resources already in place. In our previous books we've written extensively on the topic of safety and its relationship to culture. Safety done right is an example of inside strategy. But strategic thinking for performance improvement has many applications beyond safety. This book arms you with a framework of questions and ideas with which to define and measure effective value-producing behavior. This framework generates behaviors (things people actually do) that lead to results.

In Chapter 1 we ask the question: What is strategy? We take a look from diverse perspectives. We show limitations of planning and advantages of strategy.

A strategist needs to think ahead, be aware of current conditions, and imagine how small changes can lead to big effects. You'll learn how strategists from Sun Tzu in ancient China to a Greek naval strategist some 3,000 years ago thought about strategy. Why are these relevant?

Organizational perspectives today have their roots in strategic thinking of statesmen and military commanders. Strategy only started to become widely recognized in non-military organizations during the 1960s. Outside strategy looks toward possible choices of action in an ever-changing external environment. Awareness and anticipation matter. Emerging social needs, new sources of profit, competitors, changing political realities and markets, regulations, and innovations are just a few influences upon outward-facing strategies. Michael Porter, a leading authority on competitive strategy, wrote, "Strategy is the creation of a unique and valuable position involving a different set of activities."[1]

By contrast, inside strategy is a framework of choices organizations make to determine and deliver value. Inside and outside strategies are part of a whole. Behavior is dependent on what you want to achieve. Yet it's surprising how often this seemingly obvious idea can be forgotten. When conditions change, you need to question if your approach still makes sense.

If the company is about to merge, be sold off, or expand, this will influence a definition of value. And that, in turn, will determine desirable behavior. Value is context dependent. Yet searching for value from within organizations—by asking the right questions—isn't always a natural strategic impulse. But competition is.

In the late 1960s, Bruce Henderson of the Boston Consulting Group (BCG) divided his company into three units so they could compete against each other.[2] Henderson had been reading Charles Darwin and became enthusiastic about the idea of survival of the fittest. Henderson believed that competition among his red, blue, and green units would result in ever higher performance for the whole company. The blue unit headed by Bill Bain beat the other two. It did so by a wide margin and went on to form its own company. Bain and Company became BCG's biggest competitor for years to come. Be careful what you wish for.

Peter Drucker got it right when he asserted that culture eats strategy for breakfast. Strategy emerges from culture, not the other way around. Imposing a strategy without understanding the culture is asking for rejection.

A common impulse is to identify what's been successful, and do more of it—only faster. If you're successful, and you wear brown shoes on Fridays, that doesn't mean that wearing brown shoes on Fridays caused you to be successful. We see confusion between cause and correlation. Asking questions helps sort out the difference.

In Chapter 2 we ask the question: Why ask why? Strategic thinking generates questions. An organization, company, business unit, team, or individual needs responses to four overarching questions: What do you want to happen? Why do you want it to happen? How are you going to make it happen? How will you know you were successful? These questions are relevant at each level of your organization.

Questions are at the core of inside strategy. No one wants to look foolish. Yet "dumb questions" can have huge value. We like questions so much that this book contains over 500 of them. Questions sharpen awareness by helping you know what to look for. Answers frequently change. Fundamental questions remain the same. Some cultures are more open to questions than others. Your answers will vary with your unique changing circumstances. With wide-ranging stories from our own experience and research, you'll see how performance improvement generates value.

In Chapter 3 we investigate belief, motivation, and rewards. Belief drives behavior. Behavior builds (or destroys) confidence. And confidence is an integral part of mastery. But confidence doesn't happen by itself. It comes through achievement.

Like Russian dolls that fit inside each other, cultures contain subcultures. Companies, teams, and individuals operate from belief systems. Culture determines what's acceptable and what's not. Some believe that risk taking is necessary as the only way to do something new. Other cultures punish anything seen to be varying from the norm. It's important to understand organizational beliefs and beliefs about change in particular. For this reason we try to minimize perception of change when implementing strategic initiatives. If you want to change behavior, you'll need to find out which beliefs are active. Actions speak louder than words. You can recognize beliefs through observable behavior.

Chapter 4 looks at value. We make a distinction between values, those moral principles people align themselves with, and value, something that makes life better in a way that's aligned with strategic purpose. Value is always either being created or destroyed. Value destruction comes from efficiency in the wrong context. Continual value creation generates long-term success. Value is the driving force of strategic effort.

Part II, Framework, is ten short chapters, each addressing one vital strategic question in an iterative process. Every question is integral to a holistic approach to performance improvement. The ancient Greek philosopher Heraclitus wrote that you can't step into the same river twice. A framework is like the banks of the river guiding flow. The river itself is your whole system, dynamic and in constant flux. Your strategy is informed by data. The data you find will influence your decision to keep moving within the river banks, or consider alternatives.

Part III, Living Strategy, is aimed at sustaining value creation within your company. If you're short on time right now, go straight to chapter 14. However, you'll get more value from reading this book in progression.

Voltaire, an eighteenth-century philosopher and wit, said something to the effect that, if you want to speak with me, first define your terms. So, let's now turn to the question: What is strategy?

Part I

Foundations

Introduction
A new focus

Prediction is very difficult, especially about the future.
—Attributed to Nobel Prize winner in physics, Niels Bohr

Every book we've read on strategy has focused on external strategy: competition with rivals in business, or overcoming the enemy on the battlefield.

This book is different.

We take strategic thinking and give it a new focus of attention: inside your organization. This doesn't mean how to fight interdepartmental turf wars; quite the opposite. *Inside Strategy* is aimed at aligned continual performance improvement. This is an iterative process. Success breeds success. As people within your organization come to see not just the trees but the whole forest, choices and behaviors at every level become more effective.

Strategy and internal value creation are not well understood. We authors see companies simply aiming programs at problems instead of developing strategy. Strategy goes beyond problem solving. Strategic thinking is an ongoing process, a way of being and behaving. When strategy isn't understood, it's ignored. Out of sight is out of mind. Ignoring strategy leaves you rudderless. You paddle around in circles. If all your attention goes into just staying afloat, you can't think ahead. People who need strategic

Chapter 1
What is strategy?

No battle plan survives contact with the enemy.
—Field Marshal Helmuth von Moltke the Elder

Ask any two people what strategy is and you're likely to get two different answers. Ask those same two people how strategic thinking generates value at all levels from within an organization and you'll probably be met with blank stares. Ever since strategy gained currency as an organizational concept in the 1960s, there's been confusion about how to define it. Strategy isn't a detailed plan of action. Nor is it a corporate vision or an objective or a mission statement. Strategy is not what to think. It's how to think.

Business strategy aims at positioning a company for long-term value creation, profitability, sustainability, and growth. **Inside strategy's objective is value creation over time.** This definition is good. But it doesn't explain how strategy operates, and what strategy isn't. A definition may be true, but at the same time of little practical help. Everyone knows it's easy to make money in the stock market: buy low, sell high. But obviously there's more to it than that. Strategy has to answer the question: What do you want?

Surveys show what airline travelers want. They want comfort, bigger seats, a better flying experience, good food, and delightful service. There's only one problem. Few are willing to pay for all this. Henry Ford said that if he had asked customers what they wanted, they would have said faster horses. His customers didn't know they wanted cars. Steve Jobs' customers didn't know they wanted an iPhone until he gave it to them. Strategy specifies and tests a future state and then considers how to get there.

Corporate decision-makers have a bias for analysis over synthesis. The majority of these leaders come from finance and engineering: analytical minds. Seventy percent of senior executives reported that innovation is one of the top three drivers of value, according to a McKinsey survey.[3] Creativity matters. Yet most executives are disappointed with the effectiveness of their decisions. In his book, *The Fall and Rise of Strategic Planning*, Henry Mintzberg writes that planning is about analysis, and strategy is about synthesis.

Opposites attract

Synthesis is a formula for explaining change: thesis-antithesis-synthesis is a concept developed by eighteenth-century philosophers. You can think of this as a growth pattern. A child learns social behavior (thesis), goes through a teenage stage of rebellion (antithesis), and in maturity comes to reconcile opposites (synthesis). A start-up company operates by seat-of-the-pants management (thesis). But when urgency replaces importance, chaos ensues. The start-up must find ways to grow despite not having systems in place. At this stage of development there are no well-worn paths to follow. One response to this chaos is imposition of rules (antithesis). Yet too many rules and thinking is replaced by blind obedience. Then no one is allowed to ask why. You get a rigid bureaucracy. If a company is self-aware, it can learn from itself and take a new direction. It can evolve more flexible systems. This is superior functioning (synthesis). Synthesis is the creative result of combining opposites.

Strategist Carl von Clausewitz was quick to see the practical value of synthesis for reengineering the Prussian army. He spent his life in the Prussian army from the age of 12 in 1792 until his death in 1831. Clausewitz was a gifted commander and classical strategic thinker. Today he is best known as author of *On War*. Clausewitz defined war as an "act of violence to compel the enemy to fulfill our will."[4] War is a continuation of policy by other means. His book still informs military, political, and business leadership. Prussian planning and discipline generated a formidable fighting force. During the eighteenth-century Friedrich von Schrötter, a Prussian government minister, said that Prussia was not so much a country with an army, but an army with a country.

A student of Clausewitz, nineteenth-century Prussian strategist Field Marshal Helmuth von Moltke the Elder, wrote that **strategy is a collection of thought experiments and generalities rather than rules.** Von Moltke understood the need for necessary deviation, and that conditions in the moment determine options for action.

What's happening?

Understanding what's happening right now determines your options. Just because something exists doesn't mean you can see it. As Sherlock Homes put it, "The world is full of obvious things which nobody by any chance observes."[5]

There are good reasons why we can't see what's in front of us. Inattentional blindness means it's easy to see what you look for and ignore what else may be present. Expertise is a kind of filter, deep and narrow. Inattentional blindness is an expertise blind spot. In other words, to a hammer everything looks like a nail.

Goal confusion is common. A safety manager says the goal is to get workers to comply with rules and procedures. The real goal is to get workers to accurately recognize and effectively address workplace risks. A production manager thinks his goal is "maximum units out the door." But this creates quality issues resulting in rejected product and re-working. The manager thinks he's doing the right thing. What he's actually doing is reducing overall productivity. His true goal is "*quality* units out the door."

Strategic thinking can permeate throughout organizations. Senior managers determine what results should be. Middle managers below them carry out their missions. These middle managers also need to generate ideas and make choices within their own domains of responsibility and knowledge. Strategic thinkers know they must take a wider view. Developing a greater awareness of current conditions opens up new possibilities for action.

In business, project portfolio selection requires analytical skills, interpretation, and judgment. Obviously, analysis works best once you have material to analyze. But how do you know it's the right material? Analysis is reductive. It seeks to narrow options on something already existing. On the other hand, creativity expands possibilities by producing new material from which to choose. Innovation, creativity's partner, generates novel options from a unique combination of existing material, or spawns something entirely different.

When strategic formulation is the responsibility of left-brained people, the impulse is to judge, measure, and analyze. You see the limitations, right? However, the solution isn't just to give strategy formulation to the creative types, either. Right-brained people may have countless ideas, and see so many new patterns and possibilities that they may not be able to prioritize them, or adequately think through logical consequences. You need a synthesis of mindsets.

Just as no one person can understand the complexities of a large organization, no lone individual can adequately formulate strategy. Your strategy is dependent upon context, individuals, culture, and company structure. To paraphrase Sun Tzu, a Chinese military strategist of some 2,500 years ago, despite the plan, **commanders should pay attention to circumstances and adapt accordingly**. Keeping an eye on what's happening right now is essential to relevant strategy. Change happens fast. The corporate graveyard is filled with companies who failed to adapt.

***

Resources

Almost 3,000 years ago the Greeks, led by Athenians, vanquished Persia at the Battle of Marathon. They then felt optimistic. Invasion threats from across the sea had disappeared—or so they thought.

Themistocles, a politician and naval strategist, took a wider view. He understood that Athenian strength at Marathon had relied on limited and irreplaceable resources. In his view, if the enemy came back and allied itself with the Phoenicians, Athens would be overwhelmed. Themistocles understood that if this conflict arose, the enemy must be destroyed far out at sea, a new idea in warfare. What Athens needed was a stronger navy.

But opposition to his plan was stiff. And if there was one thing the Athenians liked, it was arguing. After all, they were the inventors of democracy. They also developed the essential leadership quality of rhetoric, the art of influence and grandfather of sales training. The rich didn't like Themistocles' plan because they would have to pay more tax. The middle-class didn't like the plan because it elevated the poor, those who rowed the galleys. What the Athenians were missing was a realistic understanding of their own land-based weakness. They were misreading the situation. Themistocles could see beyond the collective blind spot.

As you would expect, opponents came up with a plan of their own. Their idea was to strengthen land defenses. This was cheaper, but their real motivation was protecting social status. Opponents' plan would enhance the status of the infantry, who were drawn primarily from the middle class.

At this time a rich vein of silver was discovered at a state-owned silver mine. Themistocles used his powers of oratory to persuade the Athenians not to declare a dividend as they had intended, but to invest in shipbuilding. This was brilliant strategic thinking. The Persians did attack again. But by this time Athens was ready for them. It had 200 ships supported by another 150 from Sparta. Persuasive Themistocles had successfully sold his shipbuilding idea to Sparta, too.

An essential message from military strategists is this: **make the most of what you have**. Would Themistocles have succeeded without the fortunate discovery of silver? Unfortunately, not every strategy finds a windfall. Lack of resources and ongoing support from senior management is a prime failure point for strategic initiatives in businesses today. As my father, Mike

Galloway once advised me, "The best idea is still only an idea if it cannot be sold to management."

Fixed or fluid

For Mintzberg, planning gets in the way of strategic thinking. This is what we see in our practice, too. As we showed earlier, a plan suggests a static environment. For much of the twentieth century, this was exactly the efficient stability industry tried to achieve. But the world refuses to sit patiently still while planners make their plans. Experience of the past may inform the future, but it's unreliable as a template. As investment firms love to tell us, past performance is no guarantee of future returns. Synthesis, as a product of strategy, makes room for contingencies, those nasty things we never imagined, or hoped wouldn't happen. Strategy as a business concept has only become widespread since the 1960s. *The Concept of Corporate Strategy,* by Kenneth R. Andrews, first appeared in 1971. It's a handbook of business policy that was taught at Harvard Business School in the mid-1960s.

Andrews edited Harvard Business Review from 1979 to 1985. He was integral to the publication's success. Andrews described strategy as a pattern of decisions effective over a long period of time. Its role is to determine what the enterprise is and what it wants to be. He thought strategy should be deliberate, a view shared by Michael Porter, an authority on business competitiveness.

Porter's view

Michael Porter claims five tests for what he considers good strategy. These tests are in the form of questions. The first is primarily an outward-facing test. It measures value-proposition uniqueness. Are you offering distinctive value to your chosen set of customers at the right price?

The second test has an internal value-producing focus: a custom-made value chain. Is your set of activities the best to deliver your value proposition? And is best actually best?

When Charles Caleb Colton[6] wrote that imitation is the sincerest form of flattery, he could've been talking about best practices. As far as we know, no one has yet written the book *Great Moments in Followership* or *Obedience Training for Managers*. The trouble with careless adoption of best practice is that it limits thinking about even better options. This is why flexible and functional organizations are shifting their thinking from best practices to **better practices**. Better practice avoids the confirmation bias where we look for evidence to support what we already think. Better practices search for performance improvement, not just compliance.

In contrast with our own customer-value perspective, Porter's test continues with his competitive outlook. In our view this is a distraction from what really matters. He asks, are your activities different from your competitors'? While you shouldn't be blind to what the competition is doing, internal strategic focus is on **value delivery for the customer**. What matters is what you're actually doing, and how you're doing it. There is no one best practice because each company is different. Every company is made up of distinctive individuals. Although we may see common patterns, each cultural context is unique.

Porter's third test is about trade-offs. Again, he drives home his "uniqueness" competitive perspective when he asks, are your trade-offs different from your rivals'? As Joan Magretta writes in her book, *Understanding Michael Porter*, "Competitive advantage is not about beating rivals; it's about creating unique value for customers."[7] But the important point Porter makes about trade-offs is **deciding what you won't do.**

His fourth test is about fit across the value chain. In what way do interlinked activities enhance value? This is an excellent question which helps identify what is actually happening.

Porter's last test is holistic. It's about company stability. How much endurance does a company need to sustain tailoring the value chain, making durable trade-offs, and making activities fit over a long period of time?

Mintzberg teaches that strategy is emergent. Instead of a plan being imposed top-down, strategy emerges from interactions and behavior. **Strategy, then, is not what to think, but how to think.** And how to think depends on context.

Structures

There is no single approach to strategy that works for every organization. Strategy is dependent on the company, its ecosystem, and culture. Mintzberg identifies five types of organization: bureaucracy, professional, entrepreneurial, adhocracy, and diversified.

1. Central planning goes back at least to the ancient Egyptians. It helped them manage a vast empire. Following this model, bureaucracy became the classical structure for a business. During the Industrial Revolution bureaucracy was the dominant model. Frederick Taylor (1856-1915), a mechanical engineer, introduced "scientific management" and conducted time and

motion studies to create greater efficiencies. He saw the worker as a machine. The workforce at the time was largely uneducated. Taylor used what he saw. Workers weren't paid to think, they were paid to do. His work made a significant leap forward for efficiency and standardization. But now try selling Taylorism to millennials, the largest demographic in the current workforce, and you'll get pushback. They're better educated, and want a good measure of autonomy, plus opportunity for advancement. Machine-age industries aren't attractive to young talent. Managers of such industries struggle to understand why their workforce is not giving them the results they want. They fail to realize that the behavior of their workers is influenced by their systems. Peter Drucker, author and management consultant, warned, "Your system is perfectly designed to give you the results you're getting."

Mintzberg calls bureaucracies "the machine organization," depending upon standardization, specialization, a stable environment, task definition, and repetition. In the 1960s and 1970s when Kenneth Andrews was writing, this was the dominant model for large corporations. Deliberate top-down planning from senior management made sense. The bureaucratic organization has shaped management thinking ever since. But is this the right shape? That depends on what the organization is and what it wants to become. Figuring this out is the job of strategy.

2. Professional organizations such as hospitals and universities are complex and highly structured. They are

often conflicted between managing risk, educating students and pushing the envelope on research. They employ educated specialists who need autonomy. Administrators support professionals rather than control them. Decision making is decentralized. Consequently, in some systems, senior management has less direct power than in a machine organization.

3. Entrepreneurial organizations are generally smaller, and can be greatly influenced by the personality of the founder or CEO, often through direct supervision. Start-ups fall into this category. These organizations are flexible and adaptable.

4. An adhocracy organization pulls in expertise from various fields and requires them to cooperate. A group comes together for a specific purpose, such as making a movie or constructing a building, and then disbands. Project teams need to work together, refocus effort, and flex in a dynamic environment.

5. A diversified organization is separated into divisions that serve particular markets. It looks like a machine organization in that there is financial control from headquarters, but each division is semiautonomous.

Mintzberg's divisions are helpful but only a starting point. Every company has its own idiosyncrasies. This is why understanding a present condition should be based on close observation.

Less is more, sometimes

Michael Porter wrote that **the essence of strategy is choosing what not to do**. This idea was integral to our work[8] with AstraZeneca, a global biopharmaceutical company. They are doing a good job developing and executing against strategy. But they found themselves in a position where they needed to improve safety and quality. Defects in their quality could injure the consumer. So quality and safety must go hand in hand.

Chasing too many initiatives dilutes effectiveness. And AstraZeneca had too many of them. Our strategic process focused on a just a handful of very specific targets for quality and safety. The next year they won the Chief Executive's SH&E award. We believe this award wasn't for the 55 percent reduction in injuries (good though that was) but for a 17 point increase in pristine, first-time batches. They succeeded by doing less. Stopping activity is a problem for many managers. But tradeoffs are an integral part of decision making. You can't focus on everything. Value came from attention to what mattered as the company realized more than $30 million in savings. Our work with AstraZeneca helped them make a **shift in perspective.** It was a case of not what to think, but how to think differently.

Strategic cycles

Management guru W. Edwards Deming wrote, "If you can't describe what you are doing as a process, you don't know what you're doing." **Strategy is an iterative process.** The process moves from initial observations to understanding, uncovering value, getting agreement, prioritizing findings, identifying and allocating resources, gaining ongoing support, and measuring contribution to value. Then at this point the cycle starts again by observing a new reality. Strategic cycles of observation and change are a never-ending decision-making process. Strategizing is strategic thinking in action. Strategizing is a verb, something you do, a behavior, a perspective, and we encourage you to make it a reflex throughout your organization.

Story

Your strategy needs a story. Stories are the most powerful communication medium known. In the absence of an explanation, we humans will fill in the blanks. We make up a story—even if it turns out to be wrong. Strategy isn't going to help you change the past. It won't have an immediate impact on the present. **Strategy is about the future, a story told in future tense.**

Stories shape worldviews. Take the case of political strategy. It's aimed at persuading people to adopt a particular viewpoint. Party political strategy is a zero-sum game. Parties organize and formulate campaigns, collect resources, communicate propaganda, suppress or ignore inconvenient issues, set their own agendas, promote their own interests, and attack opponents. Political strategy views the world through a particular lens. Politics has a bad name, but without it we would have totalitarianism, or worse. Winston Churchill reportedly said, "Democracy is the worst form of government except all those other forms that have been tried from time to time."

Politics and business both rely on telling a coherent story. Stories articulate what the future might look like. Complexity, data overload, and rapid change challenge our cognitive abilities. But stories shape our thinking more than ever because they're understandable. Organizational stories must have coherence and a structure. They must be easy to understand. Stories help us comprehend and remember.

The Vanguard Group is an investment group that manages more than $3 trillion in assets. The company's philosophy is low-cost diversified investing for the long term. This idea is made clear in everything they do. Their logo is a trading ship from the time of sails. Sailing ships crossing the choppy seas is a metaphor for turbulent market conditions. "Staying the course" is their advice to investors. It's what the company is all about. Inherent in this story is the notion of risk and uncertainty. Vanguard's brand reflects their story. They're also clear about what they're not. "We believe that investing is a long-term proposition, not a matter of chasing short-term performance or investment fads."[9] Their strategy is about the long haul, but it must also make provision for short-term demand.

Strategic stories tell of what the company is trying to achieve. It could be creating what the authors of *Blue Ocean Strategy*, W. Chan Kim and Renee Mauborgne, call uncontested market space, or its opposite: competitive strategy in mature industries. Our perspective on inside strategy is not about maximizing market share, but is a way of creating value for customers, organizations, and stakeholders.

Questions

Asking the right questions is not by itself the secret of life. You have to listen to the responses. Cultures either promote or prevent asking questions. And this is why we'll now ask the question, why ask why?

Chapter 2
Why?

The art and science of asking questions is the source of all knowledge.
—Thomas Berger, author

As 2005 turned into 2006, the United States was battling in both Afghanistan and Iraq. At a fleet readiness center pressure was on to get aircraft back in the air as quickly as possible. As we toured the facility, officers told us of their struggles with a civilian contractor. We discovered that mechanics were using homemade tools to work on highly sophisticated aircraft. We asked, "Why?" No one could give us an answer. Their response was about punishment. Contractor employees were written up. We don't know who first came up with the line, "The beatings will continue until morale improves," but it's a good illustration of counterproductive behavior.

After a 30-minute conversation with these employees, we understood that they had to stand in line to check out precision tools. Moreover, that wait didn't guarantee getting the right tool. What they needed may already have been checked out. The system was working against the purpose of rapid aircraft servicing. In the absence of a workable strategy, mechanics came up with their own hidden, two-part strategy. Part A: find out who has the tool and borrow it from them. If it didn't get replaced, guess who got in trouble? Part B: if you can't borrow, make one yourself. This hidden strategy wasn't just hampering safety; it was impacting quality and flight readiness. And no one was asking why.

When employees don't think strategically about what they're doing, a company can be its own worst enemy. In the words of Walt Kelly, creator of the cartoon character *Pogo,* "We have met the enemy and he is us."[10]

Unless you've figured out how to overcome the universal laws of physics, you're stuck with reality. And that reality says that **all strategy requires tradeoffs**. You have to say no to some things so you can say yes to others. But this doesn't mean your company can't have multiple strategies. PepsiCo integrates opposing approaches. In each division one group aims at maximizing efficiency while another tries to disrupt it—before the competition can.[11]

At the same time, those strategies need to fit together holistically. **Fit is Porter's word for a value-producing activity that contributes to a stated goal.** Will it create benefit or harm? Without a holistic view, what looks like value in one area can cause damage in another. For example, some departments may find features they want in new software, but installing it causes other things to break. This happens when strategy isn't understood. Efficiencies in some areas shouldn't come at a cost to others. You can test any activity by asking what effect it will have on the existing processes.

Tony Hsieh, CEO of Zappos, is someone who is getting it right. Hsieh made company culture his number one priority. There, customer service is everyone's responsibility, not just the focus of an isolated department. Fit matters at Zappos, and we're not just talking about shoes. Hsieh wants to make sure he has the right people doing the right things.

Zappos' culture attracts employees who value service, autonomy, and fun. Zappos pays new employees $2000 to quit if they don't feel they fit in. It's an unusual strategy, and is being closely watched by the business community.

As labor markets tighten, companies compete for talent. Korn Ferry, the largest global executive search firm, declared a loss of $10m in 2009.[12] Employers now can recruit talent themselves from online sources such as LinkedIn. To meet this challenge, Korn Ferry has adopted a new talent strategy which incorporates executive search with inside strategy. This includes coaching managers, succession planning, and culture improvement. Managers are being required to develop existing employees.

Winning hearts and minds becomes ever more vital to doing the right things, and doing them right. During a client engagement, we gained a significant insight from one of Terry's questionnaires. His question was: what level of performance do employees need just to keep their jobs? We coded the responses on a scale of 1 to 10. Ten was a high-performing employee, always going above and beyond. One was somebody who was not even showing up to work. Some answers were in the 5 or 6 range. What we wanted to know was what was the company doing to move employees from 6 to 7 or from a 7 to an 8? We didn't get a lot of answers. Potential employee effort was being wasted. Strategic thinking was missing.

Strategy and strategies

Malcolm Gladwell's 2004 TED talk was called *Choice, happiness and spaghetti sauce.*[13] Gladwell tells the story of Howard

Moskowitz, psychophysicist and re-inventor of spaghetti sauce. Gladwell says that he doesn't know what a psychophysicist is. He once dated a girl who was studying the subject and he still doesn't know. Joking aside, Gladwell says psychophysics is about measuring things.

Pepsi came to Moskowitz wanting to know how much sweetener to put in its product. He thought this was a simple enough problem. But when he looked at the consumer data, it wasn't the bell curve he'd expected. Only later did he realize that PepsiCo was asking the wrong question. The search had been for the one perfect Pepsi. He realized that the data showed clusters of preferences around different degrees of sweetness. Moskowitz had a flash of insight. The search shouldn't be for one perfect Pepsi, but different Pepsis.

In the early 1980s, Moskowitz used the same reasoning when Campbell Soup Company came to him wanting a strategy for Prego, their spaghetti sauce. Eventually the company produced not one superior spaghetti sauce, but a number of spaghetti sauces to satisfy consumers with different tastes.

The shift in thinking is away from a one-size-fits-all product to addressing individuals and their differences. Instead of thinking about a grand, overarching approach, we can think of holistic strategy: a collection of interlinked strategies for different situations. Philip Evans of BCG says the strategist must look not at the company as the irreducible unit but at the individual within the organization.[14] How do employees contribute to value and how do we accurately measure contribution? Answers vary depending upon the idiosyncrasies of the company.

The rear-view mirror

Remember math class? It's wasn't enough to come up with the right answer. You had to show how you got there by working out the problem and demonstrating your grasp of logic. You may think you're successful because you have outcomes to prove it, or maybe you just deserve to succeed because you're you. All of us can delude ourselves if we don't look closely at why we succeeded. We want success to be relevant, repeatable, and sustainable. This isn't so easy in a complex system where change is constant.

At the time of this writing, the most recent Olympic Games were held in Europe. Unless we were willing to stay up half the night, on this side of the Atlantic we had to watch events after they happened. We already knew the results before we saw the competition. Our first reaction may have been disappointment at missing the excitement and tension of not knowing who won.

But time-shifted Olympics gave us a valuable change of perspective. We could see how performance contributed to winning. In terms of inside strategy, how do you recognize effective training when you see it? If you want great talent in your organization, have you profiled what a great individual looks like and then aligned your systems for support?

Groupthink

How do you know you're chasing the right goals? Asking why can be seen as a direct threat to authority. Groups have a natural bias toward conformity. Few individuals want to be the first to challenge the status quo. People often don't want to rock the boat even when they can see what's going wrong.

Hans Christian Andersen, a Danish nineteenth-century writer, re-tells the folk tale of *The Emperor's New Clothes*. The emperor in the story is a *fashionista*. He demands to wear only the finest fabrics. He even has a different coat for each hour of the day.

Two swindlers arrive in the capital and learn about the fashion-crazed emperor. They come up with the idea of claiming they can spin thread so fine it can only be seen by people of the highest taste and intelligence. They bamboozle the gullible emperor into believing this nonsense. Not wanting to lose face, the emperor pretends to be able to see this imaginary fabric, and so then does the population. No one wants to look like a fool. The emperor, wearing his fine new clothes, marches in procession through the streets. A naïve small boy shouts that the emperor has no clothes on. The message ripples through the crowd as people take up the boy's cry. The naked emperor, suddenly suspecting they are right, holds his head high and marches on.

Discussing the undiscussable

The question why needs to be used with caution. Undiscussable topics limit realistic views of what's going on. At a large multinational, accident rates decreased as we addressed problems. But we discovered we'd reached a plateau. No further improvements were happening. We needed people on the shop floor to share safety strategies. But there was a difficulty. It was socially unacceptable for one worker to talk to another about their safety performance. This was perceived as rude and unacceptable and generated rejection. "You have no safety responsibility. Stop sticking your nose into my business."

We solved this by making some employees responsible for everyone complying with specific behaviors. First, **we identified**

a few things that would make a big difference, and then assigned individuals to go on the lookout for them.

For example, imagine you're assigned to look out for people not wearing a hardhat. What happens when people see you not wearing yours? They're far more likely to say something. "Hey, safety guy, you're not practicing what you preach." This started as kind of a joke, a friendly ribbing of each other. But it grew.

We rotated assignments. Within a year-and-a-half, we had broken down the taboo of employees not being able to talk to each other about safety. In fact, people were sharing a lot. They were turning in more ideas for safety improvement. We had made it socially acceptable. We turned the undiscussable into the discussable.

This lesson continues to serve us well in our consulting practice. We ask: what is it we are doing? It may look like the goal is to reduce accidents by focusing on behaviors, measuring, and monitoring them or simply to deliver more training. We're actually changing the culture. Safety talk and behavior becomes culturally acceptable. And this is a major value proposition: a culture where better interactions among people become the norm. This makes space for value-contributing conversations aligned with organizational needs.

Chris Argyris, author and professor of organizational behavior at Harvard University, writes that organizations may not be the basic cause of undiscussable topics.[15] It is rather the way people are socialized in relation to potentially threatening issues. Much of this deeper socialization takes place in school.

Former school teacher and author John Taylor Gatto was named New York City Teacher of the Year for three years running. Following his resignation from the school system, he wrote several consequential books highly critical of educational ideology, showing how it fails young minds.

In his book *Weapons of Mass Instruction*, Gatto relates a conversation with a principal of the richest secondary school in a New York district. In private, the principal asked Gatto if he would help set up a critical-thinking program for his students. Gatto replied that he could do that. Then he pointed out the consequences. "Why would kids taught to think critically and express themselves effectively put up with the nonsense you force down their throats?" That was the end of the interview and his critical thinking project."[16] Strategy necessitates analytical thinking and expression of ideas.

Argyris has a good point about how socialization limits potential. He writes that though the corporation may be victim rather than cause, once topics are consigned to the undiscussable category, organizations collude to keep them there. Structures discourage us from asking the question, why?

Act or react?

In our practice we see a huge problem where companies are working hard, but heading in the wrong direction. Consequently the imagined results never appear. Decision-making requires courage. Winston Churchill (once voted stupidest boy in his school) viewed courage as the first of human qualities because it guarantees all others. Sometimes decisions are wrong, but making no decision is still a decision. If you don't ask the question, "Why are we doing what we're doing?" then you're likely to be shaped by forces rather than consciously shape them.

Each of us needs to constantly ask ourselves this "why" question, key to identifying the root cause. "Why" is a question that will resurface throughout this book.

When you don't ask why, you're likely to respond to problems by redoubling your effort. But this only takes you further away from where you want to go. Like a swimmer using up precious energy against a riptide, you end up being swept out to sea. Exhausted managers are so busy reacting there's no time to consider how current actions contribute to—or detract from—delivering value. No time for strategy is a dangerous symptom of disorganization. Not having a strategy is a strategy. Your no-strategy strategy leaves you vulnerable. All you can do is react. When you're in this mode, someone else is setting your agenda and you're left trying to catch up.

Hidden influences

"It's the way we do things around here." This is a description of culture; common practice. Memes are the cultural equivalent of genes. Genes are self-replicating units of heredity. They are sets of biological instructions that determine what an organism looks like and how it behaves under certain conditions. Similarly, memes are units of cultural transmission. Memes are sticky ideas that make copies of themselves. They have no other purpose than self-replication. What does a meme look like?

You can't touch or see memes directly, but you can see the results of them. Go into a restaurant and notice the napkins folded into a cone, or into origami swans. It's fashion. It's a meme. Cute kitten videos go viral on the internet. That's a meme, too. Memes spread.

Brain researchers have likened memes to parasites.[17] When you have a tune in your head that you can't get rid of, you've been infected by a meme. Sales meetings every Monday morning may be a habit that's lost its relevancy. That's a meme. The concept of memes was popularized by Richard Brodie, former personal technical assistant to Bill Gates at Microsoft, and author of *Virus of the Mind*. Success for a meme is when it reproduces itself in a new host. If you're not aware of them for what they are, they will influence your perceptions and behaviors—and not always for your own good.

The **why** question helps you expose hidden memes and determine a clear reason for what you're doing. Is your current behavior because that's just the way it's always been? Is it received wisdom, or is it active choice? Could there be more effective alternatives? Are you copying others? Is your reason now obsolete, or is it still relevant? The more things change, the more vital it is to ask why.

Strategy is a conscious act. But culture limits strategic options. Does your culture encourage the why question, or punish it? Does culture accept failure on the road to success or will the beatings continue until morale improves?

Success trap

In ancient Rome a triumph (*triumphus*) was the highest honor bestowed on a victorious general.[18] This was a grand procession of officials, the victorious army, captured slaves, sacrificial animals, and the spoils of war. At the head of the sumptuous procession came the victor riding in his chariot. Also in that chariot was a slave holding a golden crown above the victor's head. The slave's job was to constantly whisper in the victor's ear, reminding him he wasn't a god. Success can go to your head.

History is full of examples of generals overreaching themselves. Rapidly expanding empires fail because resources are spread too thin. Borders become indefensible. Businesses can turn complacent when success becomes the new norm—until it isn't. Companies from General Foods to TWA were once riding high, but today have disappeared from the corporate landscape.

When you get what you want, do you ask why? Can you identify the cause of your success? How do you know your success isn't due to planetary alignment, dumb luck, or your fairy godmother? Are you seeing the difference between cause and correlation? **You won't know unless you spend as much effort investigating your successes as you do your failures.** When you succeed, should you do more of it? The impulse is to identify what's been successful, and do more of it, only faster.

Here's where all of us need to tread carefully. By definition, too much is more than enough. If you've realized productivity gains through certain actions, shouldn't you just do more? Your investments have increased in value, so shouldn't you just buy more? Is more better? In his book, *Management: Tasks, Responsibilities, Practices*, Peter Drucker wrote that "success always makes obsolete the very behavior that achieved it."[19]

A black swan is a rare event. But threats are a common reality. Old processes can become obsolete overnight. All of us need to be alert and continually test our reason for what we're doing right now. Perhaps the biggest threat to success is the belief that tomorrow will look like today. Sunk costs, corporate persistence, and complacency support businesses to keep doing what they're doing. Yet even the most efficient production of a soon-to-be-obsolete gizmo is not going to keep a company afloat. Asking why may seem like a dumb question, but it can deliver great value.

Dumb questions

A police traffic report shows the initialism DOA. Does this mean Dead On Arrival or Date Of Accident? It's best to ask. Experts tend to use their own language, so asking for examples or an explanation in plain English leads to greater understanding. And for the record, let's make a distinction between a dumb question and a lazy one. The former is a genuine request for clarification. It admits ignorance of a subject and is an antidote to the Curse of Knowledge (blind spots caused by assumed knowledge). A lazy question is where information is readily available, only you haven't been curious enough to find it.

Pretense of knowledge leads to misunderstanding. *Margin Call* is a 2011 movie about investment fraud at a fictional large Wall Street investment bank. In the wake of firings, an employee discovers how the firm's portfolio of mortgage backed securities is exceeding historic volatility levels. Because of overleverage, the firm is on track to lose more than its market capitalization. The drama unfolds over a 36-hour period in meetings of increasingly senior executives. Eventually the CEO, played by a Mephistophelian Jeremy Irons, arrives in the night by helicopter. He's clearly the brightest and most formidable guy in the room. He sits at the head of the boardroom table and asks to have the situation explained to him as if he were a small child.

Dallas Cowboys owner Jerry Jones said, "I did my best work with the Cowboys when I didn't mind sounding stupid asking the question."[20] Questions uncover assumptions: beliefs that may or may not be accurate or functional.

Chapter 3
Belief

You can observe a lot just by watching.

—Yogi Berra, baseball manager

Belief drives strategy. Strategy drives behavior. Behavior drives results. Strategy's first concern is to define your purpose. The question is, "What do I want?" Wanting is an emotional experience. Rationalization comes later. Thousands of years ago, Socrates said that the unexamined life isn't worth living. Examining assumptions is vital because your perspectives, expectations, and behavior are determined by what you believe. Before you try to influence other people's beliefs, it makes sense to follow Socrates' advice and examine your own. We're not talking here about religious or deep personal convictions, but beliefs about your own default perspective, behavior, and habits. This means your truth about what you want, what your activities should be, what you should be measuring, customer satisfaction, reliability, safety, operational excellence, and especially what success looks like for you.

Trying to understand your own beliefs by yourself is like attempting to see your own eyeballs. Athletes and executives improve performance through coaching. Writers get a second pair of eyes from editors and proofreaders. Patients feel better informed when they seek a second medical opinion. Like the grit in the oyster that produces a pearl, a different perspective can generate new sources of value.

So we start with the difficulty of seeing ourselves. Then, to make matters worse, when we associate only with like-minded people, it's easy to develop group blind spots. Companies employing people from the same educational or experiential backgrounds may cultivate great efficiencies and deep expertise, but at the same time run the risk of groupthink. Culture is shared belief. Despite minor individual differences, **effective companies are able to gain general agreement among diverse minds about what matters– and what doesn't.** And that's why getting buy-in matters. You may think you have agreement, when in fact you don't. Better check.

***

Shawn: An industrial client engaged us to implement process improvement at two of their locations. The first engagement was a great success. Performance and culture improved. We worked well with union representatives. We made sure we had stakeholder buy-in.

During our initial assessment we tour the facility with the plant manager. Out of the corner of my eye I see a man in front of the union board. He's forcibly posting something on the wall. He's glancing over giving us dirty looks. I circle back after he leaves. He's posted anti-consultant, anti-improvement propaganda. I ask questions. What I find out is this: two days before our arrival a favored employee was unfairly disciplined. The HR manager could have acted more supportively. He didn't. Propaganda can be a means of push-back. Toxic belief is now pervasive: anything management supports, we don't.

Our strategy became active involvement. Both sides came to better understand each other. Two days later, the union president and plant manager were working together on how to make business improvement process successful. Three years later, a shop steward involved in the collaborative effort applied and got the job of maintenance supervisor. The plant manager was so impressed with this individual he was later promoted to maintenance department manager. Good things come from stakeholder buy-in.

At the client's second location, only 45 miles away, the story isn't at all the same. Location 2 engages us to do something similar. This, too, is a union-represented site. It has similar processes. It experiences similar challenges. They were aware of our business process improvement called Observation-Based Safety. They wanted that, too.

I said, "Let's not start with that. Let's have some conversations with the union. Let's talk to people. Stakeholder involvement is critical." As I talked with union officials, I discovered a toxic belief. They hate their association with the sister location because they compete for clients—even though they're in the same company. In Chapter 2 we showed how a belief in internal competition among business units backfired.

Each of these two locations had distinct cultures. Location 2 viewed Location 1 as rivals. They saw value in observation-based safety process yet they wanted to call it something else. Appearing different mattered. They wanted assurance we wouldn't use that name. They wanted input into the design. I said, "No problem." The union agreed to discuss the process, voted on it, and got back to us in about a month.

I returned the following month. As I was going into a meeting, one of the unions officials said, "There you are, the snake-oil salesman!" What's going on? I thought to myself. I called a manager to try to find out. Then I saw what had happened. Outside the entrance was a sign welcoming Shawn Galloway back to help implement "Observation-Based Safety." That was a big blunder! Location 2 has since shut down because management was so inept. The first location was a success. We found common purpose. A key reason the second location failed is because management couldn't pay attention to existing beliefs.

***

Getting buy-in is critical to success of any intervention, especially with unions and safety issues. Most unions in the United States were formed in response to wages and unsafe working conditions. Some beliefs you can change, others you can't, at least not rapidly. It's best to check.

Beliefs in common

Imagine being told this in an interview: We're looking for people to start at the bottom– and stay there! How would you feel? Alienation causes resentment. To get aligned cooperation, leaders must win hearts and minds. Employment is a behavioral rental contract. Everyone is expected to show up for work, do their best, and align themselves with cultural norms. Belief is emotional, tenacious, and drives behavior. When feelings run high, belief can even defy evidence and logic. If you're going to execute your strategy, align employees' thoughts and actions in the direction you want to go.

Show people the value of what they do and how it affects the collective purpose. Southwest's founder Herb Kelleher was clear about why his airline exists: "To make a profit, achieve job security for every employee, and make flying affordable."[21] These three concepts–profit, security, and affordability–are easy to remember, and therefore sticky.

On one occasion an executive at Southwest surveyed airline ticket pricing and asked Kelleher for a fare increase. Kelleher said, "You don't understand. We're not competing with other airlines. We're competing with ground transportation."[22] The executive misunderstood the low-fare rationale. His idea didn't align with strategic, long-term affordability so it got nixed. Four and a half decades later, low fares are still at the heart of Southwest's strategy. A Southwest pilot in Dallas came up with a plan to give employees a reason to believe. His brainchild called for the finance department to show employees profit per flight. Break-even number of customers per flight was 74.5[23]. This meant that only after passenger number 75 came aboard did the flight make any profit. Employees now had a concrete understanding of what success looks like: the minimum required to be done to pay their wages.

Southwest's culture goes far beyond fulfilling minimum requirements. Performance leads to profits, so customer service for Southwest is where each employee can make a difference. Treating customers well keeps them coming back. Everyone in the company "gets it."

Confidence

Kelleher focused on creating an environment for employees to believe in themselves. Confidence matters. Confidence is a strategic advantage, with a direct relationship to effective action. People must be able to articulate ideas simply and quickly. **Good ideas poorly expressed never see the light of day.** Potential value is lost. Organizations are fast-paced (with some exceptions). Impatience is a common characteristic. When you improve your company's operational effectiveness, you're able to capture more outside value. Effective employees are confident in their abilities. Rules, policies, and rigid approaches have limited use.

Being here

No discussion of inside strategy can ignore culture. This means recognizing existing beliefs: where you are right now. As you probably know there are some people who will ask for directions and others who can't—or won't. This reminds us of a story about a couple of tourists lost along a fog-bound, single-track road in County Kerry, Ireland. They had passed the same spot more than twice when the woman spies a farmer tending his sheep. She rolls down the passenger window of the rental car.

"Sir, do you know the way to Carragh Lake?" asks the woman.

"I do," says the farmer. There follows a long silence.

"Is it easy to get to?" asks the woman.

"Oh yes," said the farmer, not given to unnecessary chit-chat.

"We'd like to go there. Can you tell us the way?"

The farmer takes off his cap, scratches his head, and considers the question. "Well, the trouble is you're starting in the wrong place. You shouldn't start from here at all. No. It's much better to start from somewhere else. Then it's quite easy."

The moral of this story: if you want to get to your destination, it's crucial to know where you are right now. The first step in aligning people to your purpose is to understand dominant operational memes; in other words, **what beliefs are active?**

Know thyself

In this story we'll call our hero Jim. Jim's job is to monitor facilities, audit safety processes, and check for compliance. He wants employees to perform well. He believes in his mission. He thinks himself to be a reasonably good coach. Jim often hears "Charlie 223" broadcast over the factory sound system as he is making his rounds. He never much pays attention to it until one day an employee pulls him aside and says Charlie 223 is code for "safety guy on site." In Jim's mind he's a coach, but the collective belief is different. Employee teams see him as a cop.

At a Midwestern manufacturing plant, all employees take Myers-Briggs Type Indicator assessments (MBTI). This assessment isn't used to rank, typecast, or judge people. The goal is to make teams more effective by teaching them about themselves. This fosters better communication for individuals and teams. Taking MBTI or a similar assessment gives employees insight into their communication preferences. Just because you say something doesn't mean it's been heard or understood. Marital bliss aside, most people's domestic lives attest to this truism. Like Jim, many manufacturing employees are shocked at the mismatch between self-perception and how other people see them.

Common beliefs show up through observable behavior. At an energy company, linemen work on powerlines while their supervisor sits hidden in his truck watching them through binoculars. He's waiting for them to screw up so he can drive over, lights flashing, and give them a piece of his mind. Later, the linemen devise a strategy of their own. While some distract the supervisor, one lineman pops the hood of the supervisor's truck and puts reflective tape on the inside of the grill. Then from their high perch, the linemen can see at a distance the light reflecting from his truck. They now know when he's watching–and when he isn't. We call this malevolent compliance.

The operational meme here is distrust, "us against them;" a battle with winners and losers. You'll never be excellent at anything when you just fulfil your obligation to minimum compliance. What do people do when no one is looking? Answer this question and it tells you much about the culture.

People process and understand information in remarkably different ways. Some of us prefer a step-by-step approach where understanding sequence makes us feel clear about where we are, and where we're going. Others of us prefer to see the big picture and we'll join up the dots ourselves. These two preferences have been called sequential and simultaneous thinking. One person prefers detailed directions. Turn left at the bank. Go 900 feet down the road. Turn right at the post office, etc. Other people just want to see where they are on a map and chose a route themselves. We're not saying one is better, just that they are two different ways of processing information: two beliefs about communication.

***

TERRY: I learned that as a technical writer you have to speak the language of your audience. This piece of audience-analysis wisdom is what every technical writer learns. You have to know who you're writing for, and why they would be interested in what you have to say. You have to use their language. People understand things in their own ways. Here's what happened to me. I wanted to present a new idea for safety to the board of directors of a Fortune 100 company for which I was the director of training. My boss at that time had a master's degree in psychology. I showed him my research on B.F. Skinner and his associates, and my follow-up work. My idea was to create relevant technology based on behavioral science. My boss thought it was a marvelous idea. He said, "I'll get you five minutes before the board."

When I came into this meeting, I started talking about Skinner, behaviorism, psychology, and the direction of behavioral science. The reaction was dumb stares. They thanked me and said they would get back to me. Afterward, my boss collared me in the hallway. "Boy! You blew it," he said.

I realized my mistake. I had failed to ask myself the right question. Who are these people that sit on the board? Every one of them came from a financial background.

Three months later, my boss got me another five minutes. This time I spoke finance. My presentation was about safety: is it a cost center or a profit center? It's a cost center. You don't make any money out of safety. So how do you manage a cost center? You control the cost. I said I have an intervention that could reduce the cost by 40 to 80 percent. I gave them a low-cost budget to experiment with in one business unit. I asked what if we could reduce accidents by 40 percent and maintain that for three years. Would that be a good ROI? Now everybody was going wild with the dollars and cents.

They were so enthusiastic they said, "Go pick us five locations that really have different challenges." Ultimately I got 42 beta-testing locations. I achieved this by realizing we don't all process information the same way. I began speaking the language of the people I was talking to. I could see the reaction of two different belief systems: dumb stares or enthusiasm.

***

You can't always get what you want

But sometimes you get what you need. There is a third certainty in life beyond death and taxes: regulations. We worked with a large paper company for many years. Their global health and safety department came up with their own motto for the group. These guys were mostly advocates and advisors. Business units were the ones to set mandates. When the safety department looked at their real mission, they came up with a phrase *to continuously improve the quality of life of the employees on and off the job*. This had nothing to do with numbers, rates, or risk.

Any new course of action could then be tested by asking a qualifying question. In this case it was, "Does it continuously improve the lives of employees on and off the job?" Sometime the answer has to be no, because you must comply with regulations. This may mean what you're about to do is going to make employees' lives more difficult. The strategic question has to take into account the regulatory environment. But how do we minimize pain? Understanding the "why" helps. **People need a reason to believe**. In difficult times this means appropriate responses to market downturns. You don't have to react by making, say, a 20 percent cut across the board. If you have to make staff reductions, use a scalpel, not an ax. Strategic thinking is the antidote to the blunt instrument.

Crude responses to complex situations are not new. The Athenians won a naval battle against their Spartan enemies at Arginusae in 406 BC. The news in Athens was met with joy and celebration—at first. Only later did citizens learn that a storm had prevented rescuers from picking up the dead and injured out of the water. Greeks took disposal of war dead as a matter of honor.

44

Eight Athenian generals were summoned back to Athens to account for their actions. Two fled. They knew what was coming. The other six were executed in a fit of impulsive rage. This is culture eating strategy for breakfast—and getting indigestion. At that time, the Greek military had only 10 generals, so they had just destroyed 60 percent of their institutional knowledge and alienated a further 20 percent. A year later, with their strategic and military intelligence in ruins, Athens fell to the enemy.

Sometimes you can't avoid pain, but you don't have to shoot yourself in the foot. In troublesome economic times, when layoffs seem the only alternative, be sure to ask **what knowledge or capabilities are likely to be lost?** What human and capital resources will your organization need in the long-term? When marketing and customer services are bled of resources, business goes into further decline. This vicious cycle can spiral out of control. Reason must be tied to function.

Reality check

Our beliefs about the future may be wildly inaccurate. Wishful thinking can get the better of us. According to a survey by the Employee Benefit Research Institute, 10 percent of the American workforce expects to retire by the age of 60. Actually, figures show that only 36 percent have stopped working by the time they reach 60. Microsoft believed business users would embrace touch-screen desktop operating systems. They didn't, hence the roll out of Windows 10. And despite his famous five-force strategic model, Michael Porter's consulting firm filed for bankruptcy protection in November of 2012. Beliefs need a reality check.

Denial does work—until compound consequences become impossible to ignore. Then it's too late. Beliefs about where to allocate resources are based on perceived risk and reward. For example, catastrophic events easily capture our attention. According to the U.S. Department of State, only 17 United States citizens were killed in acts of terrorism *worldwide* in 2011.[24] Yet **hidden and slow incremental damage can have much greater long-term impact.** The Centers for Disease Control and Prevention estimate about 610,000[25] people die from heart disease each year. Putting off difficult, transformative decisions is all too common. We need courage to make short-term trade-offs for a long-term reward.

What you want people to do must be married to *their* reasons for doing it. Incentives do work. Alfie Kohn in his book *Punished by Rewards* asks the question: Do rewards motivate people? Absolutely, they motivate people to get rewards. Are those behaviors adding or detracting from strategic direction? Do they make sense? Punishment and reward motivate up to a point. Remove them and motivation declines, unless there are stronger emotional beliefs in play. Sustainable performance improvement requires much more than simply saying, "Do this, and you'll get that."

Management psychologist Abraham Maslow wrote our "capacities clamor to be used."[26] According to Maslow, healthy individuals want to stretch themselves and achieve their potential. This is what he called self-actualization, a high stage of personal development. All of us need confidence to maximize our own agency and effectiveness. Are people being compensated for the right things? Do they understand the "why?" **What's the belief here?**

Chapter 4
Value

Knowledge is of no value unless you put it into practice.
—Anton Chekhov, physician, playwright, author

If a tree falls in a forest and no one is around to hear it, does it make a sound? This riddle has kept philosophers stroking their long white beards for many years. It's a thought experiment about observation and knowledge. If you don't see value, does it exist? Maybe not, because when you can't see value in doing something, you're not likely to act. But there may be value that isn't immediately apparent, so it's worth taking a long, hard look.

For the sake of clarity let's make a distinction between values and value. Values come from your beliefs, and inform principles. Principles are a guide to conduct. So what is value? It goes beyond technical definitions such as return on invested capital, cash flow, market expectations, and management skill. Our definition is broad: **value makes life better in some way that's aligned with overall strategic purpose**.

Seeing value
When it comes to work orders, safety usually takes precedence in most organizations. But at one manufacturing plant, some people believed priority should be given to production work orders. A production work order calls for replacing malfunctioning machinery which could cause quality problems or a slowdown in production. This has nothing to do with employees getting hurt.

47

We discovered, based on an incorrect perception, that production took priority over safety concerns, a few people were taking advantage of the system by writing up production work orders and labeling them as safety issues in the hope they would be taken care of sooner.

When managers started tracking cycle time, which measures from initiation to closure of a work order, they found safety orders actually closed much faster than production work orders. With data disproving the production-priority belief, the company knew it needed to change its value perception.

The first thing management did was to list work orders, including status and completions. They posted the data on the bulletin board for everyone to see. But naysayers still believed production was the most important thing. When they saw the posted data, they responded by saying, "Well, that was last month."

On a subsequent visit to the facility, we saw something remarkable. Instead of stapling each new closed work order status over the previous one, they hung the new data sheet below the previous one. The bulletin board had lists reaching down to the floor.

Everyone could now see ongoing data showing that safety cycle times were indeed faster than production ones. Showing this data *over time* caused people to change their beliefs. It had to be seen to be believed. Value perception matters.

***

At a large multinational corporation, the vice president of environment, health, and safety (EHS) has a global map in front of him. He's overlaying visual data displaying where most of their problems occur. What he sees is a correlation of safety problems with the economically poorest areas. When he shows us this, we think of Ruby Payne, an educator who works with disadvantaged public schools in very poor neighborhoods. We bring her in as a consultant. Ruby's experience has taught her that children from resource poor backgrounds are not necessarily learning disabled. They just learn in a different way. And here is where she shines a light on value. Disadvantaged children tend to learn from specific to general. The problem is that most education goes from general to specific. These children need a concrete example first, and only then an abstract generalization. What works for children also proves to be the case for adults. We put this knowledge to immediate practical use in the workplace. We modify how we deliver safety training in these geographic areas and get fantastic results. One small change led to a large increase in value.

Deep value

Deep value keeps on giving. It's a long-term proposition. Deep value is like a springboard propelling you to ever greater levels of future capability. Results may not be immediately apparent. While you're building your springboard, it may look like a cost. But you're investing in a better tomorrow. Only when it's functional can you leap off into new futures.

Deep value has a long history. In 14th century Portugal, a new ship design changed everything. It was called the carrack. For the first time, this three- and four-masted ship design made long sea voyages possible. Christopher Columbus sailed across the Atlantic in a carrack. Five years later, Vasco da Gama circumnavigated Africa on his way to India in such a ship. Previously, merchants had to travel overland the vast and hazardous trade routes between Europe and China. The maximizing effect of deep value made it possible for merchants to open up new and faster trade routes with Asia. The new ship design meant greater value was assigned to sea power. Trade increased. Perspectives and expectations changed. European wealth followed. This design change created deep value for the next 400 years.

Deep value came about in the early 1960s with research into packet switching, a digital network communication method. This technological event made it possible to connect computers, laying the foundation for the internet. As we all know, the internet has a life of its own, creating an unprecedented impact on just about every area of functioning.

Today, new understanding of the microbiome, colonies of complex microorganisms that make up the human and animal environment, is revolutionizing medicine. But deep value doesn't have to come from earth-shaking discoveries. Deep value is relative to its context. All it has to do is have a long-term positive effect. This can be as simple as replacing a shirt button.

SHAWN: I used to take my shirts to be laundered at a discount drycleaner. Their shop is about twenty minutes from my home. Occasionally they would leave small stains on my shirts. When I pointed this out to them I could tell they didn't really care. When I was pressed for time, I got my shirts laundered at MW Cleaners, which was closer, more convenient, but more expensive.

One day I dropped off a shirt that I didn't realize was missing a button. When I got the shirt back from MW Cleaners I noticed a small tag attached. It said, "In accordance with our quality process we replaced this button for you at no charge." This is a good example of creating deep value by delighting customers. I posted a picture of their tag on Facebook. I plan on being their customer for a long time to come.

Value has size. It can be large or small. Strategically, identifying and describing value shows us where we should put our energy. What does value look like for you? What adds value to your organization? What adds value for your employees? What creates value for your customers? Have you asked them?

***

Creation

Here's an example of how strategic thinking creates value. Our client organization is a hospital. In the physicians' lounge, meals are catered on gold plates. Nurses are dissatisfied with their compensation and the long, unpredictable hours they must work. Their lifestyle suffers. Despite the sumptuous dining room for the physicians, the hospital can't see its way to giving nurses more money. A small raise would be perceived as an insult.

We poll the nursing staff about their frustrations. We ask what value looks like. Their primary concern is to get a life. They particularly need good daycare for their children. They need time for personal and family responsibilities such as physical fitness, going to the bank, daily chores, and school activities.

The hospital has its own daycare center. It has a fitness center for cardiac patients. Yet both the daycare and fitness centers are underutilized. Our recommendation: a zero raise, but access to daycare and fitness centers, and compensation time for personal activities. Nurses go for it. They're thrilled. The goodwill value created for the hospital far outweighs the small scheduling costs.

51

At the time of this writing, we're working with another hospital system to help them strategize about the rapidly changing future. Where will the value be for all stakeholders? What changes and behaviors are likely to deliver value? How can everyone have a better experience?

What we know for sure is that the hospital model we use today will soon be a thing of the past. Forward-thinking hospitals are not just looking for how they will compete with existing rivals. The conversation isn't only about cost. They're looking at new ways of creating and delivering value. They see a bigger picture and how it constantly changes. With information about costs and patient outcomes available, performance expectations change. Well-informed consumers shop for services online. When power shifts, so does value. Patients' choices are expanding. The quality of their experience matters. And the emotional component of experience weighs heavily in decision making: hearts and minds again.

New or developed **capabilities** lead to new opportunities for value creation. **Value creation is the blue ocean of inside strategy.** For example, almost all sleep problems result in performance deficit.[27] Scientists have discovered how the blue light emitted from smartphones, tablets, and computer screens can cause retinal damage, and disrupt the circadian rhythms of the body's internal clock. If you're reading a backlit screen late at night and then you can't sleep, it may be because of blue light. New value is created with counter measures. In this case, optometrists are providing blue-blocking glasses for evening use. Developers create software such as f.lux to block blue light.

Value opportunities are being created all the time. Can we see ours? Developing foresight means becoming alert to possibilities. The question is a playful one: What if?

Value destruction

In 1942, Joseph Schumpeter coined the term "creative destruction" to describe the cycle of demolition and renewal. Value is destroyed when it's not replaced by something better. Causes may be misplaced strategic choice, having too many initiatives, not allowing enough time for a process to unfold, impatience, unrealistic thinking, insufficient leadership insight and commitment, lack of courage to stay the course, risk avoidance, short-term thinking, cultural limitations, focusing on the wrong things, misaligned incentives, mistreatment of employees, disrespect, false urgencies, and emotional blind spots.

Even efficiency can destroy value. We'll go into that one in the next chapter.

Value is lost by simplistic thinking. You can solve a problem to unwittingly introduce five more. **Accountabilism** is adding one layer of accountability on top of another because the first one didn't work. People ask us if you can be too safe. The answer is "Yes."

Ridiculous rules destroy value. There's an OSHA requirement that when you pass under any kind of danger, you have to wear a hard hat. This generally makes sense. But at one site people go for 25 or 30 miles out in the open, and then go under an underpass. On one occasion a man was caught not wearing his hardhat. The company chief made a rule that everyone must wear a hardhat at all times. Have you ever tried going to bed in a hard hat? We thought not. Walk a 25 mile stretch in a hardhat on a hot summer day and it can boil your brain. The wear-a-hard-hat-all-the-time rule is a value destroyer. It treats people like children, and then resentment kicks in.

Value destruction happens when people are alienated. When no one is leading, value goes into decline. When this happens, people will comply with rules, but ignore the intention. This is the polar opposite of strategic alignment. Sometimes managers are too vague in stating what they want, or they don't think through consequences. They've failed to win hearts and minds. You can't force consensus; it has to be earned. Dumping data on employees is not an answer.

Engineers love data. But it does little for the average worker in a plant. Too much shared data with lower-level employees is just overload. Many companies, rightly, try to keep people informed. What they may not realize is that the message has to change for different levels in the organization. What's appropriate for a CEO and direct reports is different from what middle managers can use, from what first-line supervisors need to know, or what the average worker will respond to. Information has to be tailored to the user. Asking a machinist to boost productivity by six percent is like asking a private to plan a battle. Knowing the "why" is good. But people need to understand the "how." When you want to disseminate the same information to various levels, it has to be at different levels of detail. An unfiltered data dump destroys value.

There is also the value-destroying problem of silo or departmental turf protection. We helped a client realize that their employees needed more training. The company responded by setting up a hastily constructed training. However, when employees were asked how effective the training had been, most said it was boring, awkward, and had little practical use. Instead of finding out what employees needed to help them contribute value, the new training department had a death hold on the training agenda. Trainers chose the topics, and how they would be delivered. The training department saw its objective as delivering training. Value had not been included.

We convinced the director of training to ask questions of the other departments: What would be valuable to their employees? How could training be most effectively delivered? Responses to these questions differed widely. After meeting initial resistance, the trainers came to understand that their responsibility went beyond just delivery. They saw that the people they train are their customers. Their department needed to offer value-producing topics delivered in acceptable and understandable ways to its employee-customers. Over time, and with encouragement from senior management, the training department transformed from a rigid silo to a responsive partner with other departments.

Use your data

Employees observe the work of others during an observation-based safety process. They're looking for risky behaviors compromising safety, quality, and productivity. Initial results are good. Performance improves. Then management makes an error by falling into the trap of thinking more is better. They want employees to make and record more observations. They want as many as possible. There's a boost in performance. Then it tapers off. Management responds with more rules. It becomes mandatory for everybody to perform the observations, but there's no improvement in performance. Cash incentives are dangled in front of employees to boost their observation count. Observations increase, but performance doesn't.

After a couple of years, they call us in to find out why. We discover employees are leaving the name of the observer blank and trading completed observation forms like baseball cards. We dig deeper. At first people were indeed looking for improvement opportunities. They identified issues so nobody would get injured or upset a process. This was a proactive intervention and everyone saw value. They wrote observations believing that somebody was paying attention and would make changes. But changes weren't made. Employees felt their valuable observations were going into a black hole. Was management paying attention? Employees started writing names of Disney characters on their observation forms. This went on for several months and validated their worst suspicions. Nobody was looking.

When management discovered they had no record of employees by the name of Donald Duck, Goofy, and Mickey Mouse, the creative writers were in trouble. More rules ensued. One of them was: you must turn in observation forms to your supervisor at the end of shift on Fridays. The threat for noncompliance was discipline. But no disciplinary action actually ensued. This validated that what mattered to management was only the numbers.

They wanted numbers. That's what they got. This is an example of the Hawthorne effect: a reactive response to being observed. An increase in attention changes behavior. Initially it boosts productivity. But the effect is short-term and resource hungry. As soon as attention flags, so does productivity. We knew quantifying observations wasn't enough. We had to improve the process by actually doing something useful with the collected data. After several months, we turned the situation around.

Management's simplistic thinking was destroying value. Simplicity is a worthy aspiration, but you can have too much of a good thing.

The enemy within

Some value-destroying problems will always be with us. Then it's a case of trying to limit harm. Treat people well, get their buy-in, give them a sense of value contribution, and you're less likely to encounter dangers from the enemy within: fraudsters, thieves, and vandals. These people can cause havoc from the inside of an organization. According to a 2013 poll[28], about 70 percent of senior executives report at least one incident of fraud. Some fraudsters were previously star performers. You'll probably remember the case of Nick Lesson who caused the collapse of the Barings, a merchant bank. He made unauthorized risky trades. The result was a loss of $1.4 billion.[29]

Thieves partner with people on the inside to destroy value by stealing technology and information.

Value destruction from vandalism can have even more dire consequences. Disgruntled employees can ruin a company's hard-won reputation. In 2012, a fast-food employee posted pictures of himself online wearing dirty shoes standing in a tub of lettuce. The caption read, "This is the lettuce you eat at Burger King."[30]

Reputation is difficult to establish and easy to destroy. While there will always be rogue employees, performance improvement starts early with winning hearts and minds. You don't want to shut the barn door after the horse has bolted. Organizations need to take consensus building seriously.

Neglect

Value can be eroded through a false perception of success. This leads to dangerous complacency. Management by exception assumes the absence of identifiable problems means all is well. This shows up through starved resources. What you think is robust becomes vulnerable.

The case of the Y-12 break-in grabbed the attention of media. Y-12 National Security Complex in Oak Ridge, Tennessee was built as part of the secret Manhattan project during World War II. Today, it's the only site in the U.S. devoted to fabrication and storage of weapons-grade uranium.[31] After the September 11, 2001 attacks, the Highly Enriched Uranium Facility was constructed to safeguard uranium at a cost of more than half a billion dollars. Five hundred security officers with licenses to kill guard the place aided by military grade firepower.

In July of 2012, an eighty-two year old nun and two comrades in their late fifties and early sixties managed to break into the secure zone. They weren't planning to make a nuclear bomb, or commit acts of terrorism. They were peace activists. They cut through fences, climbed obstacles, and found no resistance. Their mission was to spray paint messages of protest, which they did. A camera that should have warned security wasn't working. Their Plowshares organization has demonstrated lax security at other nuclear sites, too. Without these activists, criminals with less benign intentions—and results—might have alerted us.

Lack of investment in maintenance is faulty thinking. When productivity takes precedence over safety, which corners are being cut? What new risks loom large? If you don't maintain your vehicle, it may run just fine, until it doesn't. What value is being eroded by neglect?

Adding value

At one time, jeans with holes in them would be thrown out. Now they've become fashion. Value addition is a matter of perception and creativity.

At the time of writing, we're helping a hospital system learn from Disney, an entertainment company. Healthcare organizations can apply Disney's customer service methods to improve patient stays. Disney's focus is to give their customers experiences that keep them coming back, the sort of service they'll tell friends and family about. When you go on a Disney cruise, servers actually remain with you throughout your entire voyage. They're also not trying to fleece you for every imaginable add-on. There are lessons here for hospitals. For Disney, it's all about customer experience, from the check-in process, all the way to returning home. The hospital system we're working with is looking at value contribution, and value from the perspectives of patients and employees. They have 25,000 employees and they don't want to lose physicians to other organizations.

Patient or guest experience is a felt experience. **New value is discovered by improving old perceptions.** The idea of patient as disease (the hernia in bed five) is giving way to treating people as whole individuals, the way Disney treats their guests. Disney's "chain of excellence" starts with leadership, how leaders take care of cast members (their name for employees), and how cast members take care of guests. Disney has solved logistical problems that are common to hospitals. For example, behind the scenes resort management, such as laundry, parking, and housekeeping are common to both industries.

Here's an example of how value creation can be translated into different contexts. Terry once asked the CEO of a major company to tell of a recent success. He replied, "I got those little round tables out of the breakroom and replaced them with big, long tables." Why was this a significant accomplishment? "I'm getting people to talk to each other who never talked to each other before. I'm doing it with meetings, too. We're seeing great value from forging new interpersonal connections."

Performance value

I don't want any yes-men around me. I want everyone to tell me the truth, even if it costs them their jobs.[32] This witticism is attributed to Samuel Goldwyn. There's almost always a gap between what the leaders think is happening and what's really happening. Beyond the fear factor, there are legitimate reasons why leadership can't directly communicate and learn what's really going on. This reminds us of the old joke that a consultant comes to your office, looks at your watch, and tells you what time it is. All the information we give to leadership comes from their employees. **We don't coach for results; we coach for performance.**

Performance enhancement is an ongoing process leading to greater ability. When customer service delights customers, they come back for more delight. When people value what they do and the organization they work for, an attractive environment is created where people want to work.

Performance value improves processes. It fosters new or more useful capabilities. Those, in turn, generate new options. One definition of wealth is having options.

Think of how a golfer or tennis player acquires skills. In the beginning, it's about how to hit the ball. This requires mental focus. All attention is fixed on connecting with the ball. But over time, a player builds muscle memory. The golf swing or tennis stroke becomes automatic. This reflexive movement uses a different part of the brain than it used to acquire the skill. The brain has grown new connections to handle this new skill set. Cognitive space is freed up for the next important element— where you want to hit the ball, otherwise known as strategy.

Fail or focus

Value creation means tradeoff. A few small changes can make a huge difference. But they have to be the right changes. You need to know which performance to improve. Without being specific, it's impossible to know where to focus effort. Surviving businesses soon learn that competing on price is a dangerous strategy. Fail to identify what value is, what it means, how it operates, and you won't be around long. Inside strategy must continually evolve toward greater value-producing efficiencies and effectiveness. If it isn't lean, it won't last. **Constant contribution to value is the driving force of strategic effort. Long-term success only comes from a continual focus on value.**

And with that in mind, we'll now focus on the first of ten important strategic questions. Who is the customer?

Part II

Questions

In this section, we explore our framework of ten strategic performance-improving questions. As you read through the questions, you'll see how each question builds upon the previous one. The framework is iterative. As you uncover your unique situation, you may need to backtrack and reconsider prior questions in the light of newly discovered data. For example, you may identify your vision of success and then ask what's the rationale? If your rationale doesn't stand up to scrutiny, you'll need to reconsider the appropriateness of your vision.

Your responses to these questions will change over time. Interventions will have a ripple effect and cause responses elsewhere in the system. Small changes can have big effects.

1. Who are your customers?

2. What's your vision of success?

3. What's your rationale?

4. What's your story?

5. What is the scope?

6. What supports or conflicts with your ability to succeed?

7. Where's the relevant data?

8. How will you choose?

9. How will you create strategic alignment?

10. How will you sustain performance improvement?

Chapter 5
Customer

Strategy without an objective is like a broken pencil.
Pointless.
—Anonymous

Question 1: Who is the customer?

We told you this was a book about thinking. We're now going to apply a piece of mind-bending logic. Before you can deliver value to customers, you have to identify who they are.

Peter Drucker saw that the primary purpose of business is to create a customer. We generally use the term "customer" loosely to mean a consumer, client, or buyer. The ultimate customer is the one who buys goods and services from your organization. For non-profits, ultimate customers are those who benefit from the organization's mission. A customer should receive value. From an inside-strategic point of view, **customers are all of the people impacted by business processes**. People within your organization rely on each other to produce value. One person's output is another person's input. Employees may be customers of an improvement process. Supervisors are customers of line staff. Managers are the customers of supervisors. In a complex organization with multiple units, customer identification can go unrecognized. That's a problem.

During a visit to a client's facility, a plant manager proudly told us about how he had purchased brand-new ladders because employees were complaining about the rickety old ones. From the plant manager's perspective he was trying improve safe operation in his plant. After going only a hundred feet into the building we saw somebody using an old ladder. Embarrassed, the plant manager asked the employee why he wasn't using the new ladders. The employee pointed over to the locked maintenance shack where the ladders were kept.

Eventually we discovered that the maintenance manager had the key. His major concern was theft, so he ran a chain around the ladders and decided he was going to be the only key holder. He did this even though the name of the company was spray-painted on the side of each ladder.

Employees could see this was a problem, but hadn't brought it to the manager's attention. Employees were the maintenance manager's customers. What they needed were stable ladders. The maintenance manager had **failed to identify his customers** and give them what they required to succeed.

Everyone should understand what their company or business unit is trying to achieve. Everyone should know who their immediate customers are. Teams are each other's customers. Individuals within teams deliver value to each other. Four questions can help clarify:

Who will benefit from what we are doing?

What do our customers need from us?

What does the customer value?

Are we delivering the right value to the right customer?

***

Healthcare is on track to become a commodity. Value streams and financial models are about to change. The medical community makes money in new ways. Organizations now reach for a better understanding of employee engagement and customer loyalty. Many believe that within five years a person in need of an MRI will be able to pick the lowest cost provider online. Choice will be based on cost for the average consumer. Clinics and hospital groups are trying to strategically position themselves.

A major hospital system we currently work with is **investing the time** to look carefully at this ongoing question of who is the customer. At first glance, customer identification may seem obvious for a hospital administrator. Customers are patients, physicians, and staff. But there are more customers than just these few. For example, a physician-contractor may be the owner of an independent organization such as a medical testing facility. Such people are non-employee autonomous professionals with needs of their own. A hospital system may have embedded contractors such as a food service company. How do they add value? What do they need?

Like most of the healthcare industry, this hospital system is evolving fast. There are plenty of reasons: shifting paradigms, new expectations, customer demand, hot competition, and alternative opportunities for talent. It's a case of adapt or die. They have to compete on value. That means high reliability with superior operational excellence. They're paying attention to the first performance-improvement question: **Who is the customer?** Only when you answer this question can you ask what your customer needs to succeed.

The hospital system recognizes why they must identify non-obvious customers, those that may influence their business. They want loyalty from customers. They don't want nurses to leave for a different hospital. They don't want the practice-owning physician to pick up and move to the hospital down the street.

What customers value

It's not practical or possible to know everything about your customers. You do need to know what matters to them. In our workshops, we give people a hands-on exercise. If you were attending one of our sessions, we'd ask you to think about three people working directly for you. If you don't have direct reports, think about three people you work with closely. We'd ask you to write down their first names. We don't want to embarrass anyone, so you wouldn't have to share this information. But we would want you to answer this question: what do they care about? We're guessing that family members come either top of the list or near it. Now write down the names of family members of your three direct reports. If you're going to influence your customers you need to know who and what matters to them, right?

SHAWN: While working in Europe I happened to meet an American family as I was travelling on the train between Lucerne and Zürich. The man, woman, and their 12-year old daughter were living in Cairo and vacationing in Switzerland. I'll call the woman Cathy. Cathy was senior vice president of human resources for a giant, worldwide corporation. Soon the topic of conversation turned to an interest both of us share: motivation and performance.

Cathy had just returned from the United States where she had been celebrated for her help in securing contracts in some of the most difficult parts of the world. At a banquet, an executive vice president was sharing Cathy's accomplishments with the audience. As Cathy was about go up on stage, he told listeners that she had been on the road for 215 days during the past twelve months to achieve what she did. This was Cathy's moment of truth. Suddenly she realized that time missed with her 12 year-old daughter couldn't be made up. Being 12 only happens once. Cathy's daughter was a higher priority than her current job. She immediately took a lower-level job which allowed her to stay close to home. Cathy was being recognized for the value she contributed to the company, but that was in conflict with what she really wanted. **What matters to your customer, matters to you.**

***

A constant question

There's a cartoon where the husband and wife are at the breakfast table. He's looking up from reading the newspaper. She looks sad. The caption reads, "Seventeen years ago when we got married, I told you I love you. If anything changes I'll let you know." **'Who is the customer?' is a question that needs to be asked often.** You can't just ask this once and assume the answer or needs will always remain the same.

Who is the customer? That depends. **The customer changes with circumstances.** One important circumstantial change is progress. Our work with a number of CEOs is to help them understand why their group of companies needs to make strategic changes. Once we get alignment and unified support, the customer will change down to the executive staff at each business. As the executives start to understand and speak with a unified voice, then we can take the message further down into the organization. Managers' behavior needs to support the organization's direction.

Strategy starts at the top of the organization. People pay attention to the boss's agenda. While the overall vision (see next chapter) will be formulated by the organization's leadership, the first customers you may need to identify could be influential individuals with indirect power among the rank-and-file who might not have hierarchal power. They may be the best people who can understand the proposed value of a behavioral change and communicate it to their peers. In a culture of divisiveness, starting with management and supervisors can be an exercise in futility. The rank-and-file won't listen in this us-against-them culture. So the question becomes, who has the ear of the rank-and-file? These people are your customers.

Forgetting

When you don't keep asking who your customer is, it's easy to forget who they are. Then you're vulnerable to losing your way. Every organization wants to be efficient, but if efficiency takes center stage, you can lose sight of purpose. This is true with misapplication of customer-response systems. Is the system designed to help the customer or the company? Who hasn't been frustrated by interactive voice response (IVR) technology? You'd be forgiven for believing IVR systems were invented as an instrument of torture in a hot place well below ground. Such systems may be designed to use resources wisely. Yet one that irritates customers does more harm than good. When "you don't find the option you want, press 9 to return to the main menu" is likely to raise blood pressure.

So-called customer satisfaction surveys that forget to give recipients a chance to respond outside of a narrow list of options are forgetting who the real customer is. When customer service agents are rewarded for the number of inquiries they handle instead of the number of satisfied customers, they have forgotten who they're working for and to whom they should be contributing value. Internal efficiencies must be aligned with customer needs, not at the expense of them. Organizational amnesia is a dangerous condition.

Take the example of the RFP (request for proposal) method. The underlying assumption is that the RFP process will uncover a differentiator based on your selection criteria. But the most accomplished consultants, writers, or other professionals aren't interested in filling out a hundred-page questionnaire. They don't have time for a dog-and-pony show. They get work through referrals. And they're probably busy.

A common argument for RFPs is that they avoid scope creep. This is wishful thinking. As a consultant investigates the current reality, new ideas, problems, and details come to light. This is what consultants do. It's how they realize value for you. Where the RFP idea is most unproductive is that it assumes an off-the-shelf solution. It's erroneously designed to save the hard work of thinking and asking the right questions. The RFP process can second-guess and oversimplify a situation. It's like asking your doctor to prescribe before diagnosing. A better solution is to seek out the most accomplished individuals who have an established reputation. Invite them to assess your needs.[33]

What effect do your activities have on your customer? Do RFPs ignore the reality of a customer/proposer's experience? Have they correctly articulated the requirements? The IVR may be cheap, but does it infuriate or satisfy your customers? Are customer satisfaction surveys merely "happy sheets" designed to support the status quo, or do they ask for actionable feedback and suggested improvements? What matters to your customer matters to you.

The urge to merge

Cultures clash as two large organizations we work with are merged. One organization is focused on operational discipline. Rules dominate. Mistakes aren't tolerated. Employees are often reprimanded. The other organization has a different view. It believes in the capabilities and reasoning of its people. If someone makes a mistake, there's usually a good reason. This company doesn't rush to judgment or discipline.

We could see the striking differences right away. Each company had its own identity, yet now it was part of a new entity. Employees still saw themselves as belonging to their legacy company. As a counter measure, the companies adopted a new name. Yet the differences continued.

The merged organization tried putting supervisors from one company over team members from the other. Projects fail at the beginning, not at the end. There was mass confusion because of lack of initial strategic thinking.

They've now made significant progress by answering the critical questions we put before them. Who are customers? Who are your internal stakeholders? What value are you trying to provide for them? Who do you really want to be? What are you trying to accomplish?

Growing pains are to be expected when bringing together two diverse cultures. But they're getting through it by asking the right questions. The first inside strategy's performance-improvement question is **who is the customer?** Next, we'll look at **what we want to accomplish**: the vision.

Consider this...

- Who is your immediate customer?
- Who is your customer's customer?
- Which customers are you inadvertently ignoring?
- What do your customers want to accomplish?
- What matters to them that you can provide?
- How do you know what value your customers want?
- How has that changed over time?
- How will what customers' value be different in the future?
- Are you asking 'who is the customer?' often enough?

Chapter 6
Vision

The best way to predict your future is to create it.
— Attributed to U.S. President Abraham Lincoln

Question 2: What is the vision?

Decisions are easier when you have a clear vision. "Visioning" is a process that can be used for almost any future state. You probably have a personal vision for your next stage of life, your circumstances in five years, what you want to be doing, who you want to be with, what your retirement might look like. You can conjure up a picture in your mind's eye of what an ideal future looks like. Visioning is a way you invent the future. It's a hypothesis you'll need to test.

Assumptions, by their nature, are sometimes wrong. But we're going to assume you've done the work to answer the big strategic question of why your organization exists. For example, McKinsey & Company's vision is to "help leading corporations and governments become more successful." For Walt Disney, it's to "make people happy." Vision creation is usually an effort led by the group who holds the purse strings. However, **ownership and implementation is the responsibility of everyone**.

Defining vision is a design process that begins with describing success. Creative and critical thinking are necessary. You can't set strategy just with opinions. You need ideas. Then you have to test your ideas. For example, product developers create prototypes and let people interact with them. Feedback matters, but be careful with whom you share your early ideas. Vision as an untested hypothesis is vulnerable.

You must have answers if people are to believe in you. When it's time to communicate, your value proposition should be captured by a neat narrative. A clear rationale and concise story stick with customers. Generate alternative futures and then pick what makes sense. What works for one organization may be rejected by another.

We examined belief and value in Chapters 3 and 4. Will your vision be aligned with what people already believe and value, or will you need to change beliefs and perspectives? Trying out new ideas in a limited context allows you to collect data to see what works.

Understanding is not usually an abstraction. Instead, people have to be able to experience themselves acting in new ways. By collecting and examining data, you begin to see if you're moving in the right direction. Imagine the value you want to realize through trying on a range of perspectives. What could you see customers actually doing? How would executives behave differently? What changes in employee behavior would you see? What behaviors could lead to value-producing results?

Just copying someone else's vision is unlikely to give you the results you want. Why? It ignores your own organization's cultural uniqueness and distinct capabilities. Some organizations actively encourage innovation. Others only pay lip service to it. Still others are hostile to innovation and punish it. Beware of potential traps. Do you have the resources to carry out your vision? Can you create a strategy for implementing it?

Look both ways

Just like the human body, organizations continually change over time. Sometimes that change is imperceptible. Other times it can be revolutionary. Change management doesn't have to be daunting— unless you need daunting change. Communicating your own history is one way to give people a reason to believe in change. **Performance-improvement vision looks forward.** At the same time, management mustn't lose sight of where the company has been.

On July 6, 1988, an explosion killed 167 men on Occidental Petroleum's Piper Alpha North Sea oil production platform. Post-mortem analysis specific to Piper Alpha pointed to poor judgment with respect to productivity versus safety. Root causes were deeply embedded in culture and corporate structure.[34] Since then, Occidental has made progress. Crews today are unlikely to have direct experience of what led to the Piper Alpha disaster. Without a sense of history, they would baulk at having to comply with copious rules, regulations, standards, and regulatory bodies. A burning platform is no place for lengthy discussion. You need enough time for a collaborative process to define your vision at each level of your organization.

Today, Occidental Petroleum is committed to integrity: "We demand integrity and personal accountability at every level of the company with an unwavering commitment to safety and environmental stewardship."[35] This means running a tight ship. Your own organizational history and institutional knowledge will color what's desirable, what makes sense to you, and what's possible for your group. Don't just think vision; think visions.

But what does it mean to me?

Your vision will influence performance at all levels within your organization. To do that, it has to become a reality for everyone.

The University of Texas (UT) at Houston Police Department integrates its vision with those of two institutions it serves: M. D. Anderson Cancer Center and UT Health Science Center at Houston. The police department's vision is:

> To be the leader as a premier university law enforcement organization in the United States, setting standards of excellence to meet the challenges of the changing future. We will maintain our loyalty to our community and profession as we serve with pride.[36]

Well-intentioned though this statement is, it doesn't actually tell anybody what to do. The department's overall statement is necessary, but not sufficient. And they know that, which is why they go on to develop a more fine-grained version. Essentially, their vision is to create a secure environment to allow the work of the campus to proceed unhindered. The police department's vision rests upon five core values: leadership, professionalism, service, integrity, and innovation. The department explains how each of these is demonstrated in practice by actual behavior. For example, they embody professionalism by treating everyone with "dignity and compassion, reflecting a positive attitude at all times, performing with pride and commitment, and maintaining exemplary appearance at all times."

The police department's strategic goals are aligned with the organizations they serve and protect. One item in their list is to safeguard and enhance their resources. This generalized statement becomes more concrete upon further definition. They specifically itemize sub-goals. One of them is to collaborate with external agencies to reduce crime risks for the university community.

Make it real

Visible progress toward a goal is a prime people motivator. Your vision operates at every level of your organization through three vital factors: roles, responsibilities, and results. Let's say a supervisor's *role* is to be an effective communicator. His or her *responsibility* is for (you guessed it) communication. But we can't leave it there. Communication means different things to different people. By itself, the term is too vague because it doesn't say what behaviors constitute communication. So, what does communication responsibility mean for this supervisor? You need to break it down into specific behaviors, such as active listening before responding, or intervening immediately when someone is at risk. Even that intervention needs further defining. For example, sharing a concern for a person's safety, finding out why they are engaging in risky behavior, and talking with them about better alternatives. See how this makes it easy for a supervisor to imagine doing these things? It's more concrete. These behaviors lead to results. *Results,* in this example, could be greater awareness of hazards, reduced frustration, and a more functional workforce.

Be specific

Domtar Corporation operates two business segments: pulp and paper, and personal care. We worked with the paper division. The location has done an exemplary job of creating eight S.E.A.L (Safety, Excellence, Awareness, and Leadership) teams, each with their own brand, logo, vision, and mission. The idea is for all teams to come together to improve the safety of the work environment and each other. They encode this idea as 810, 8 missions + 1 outcome=safety excellence.

To keep people safe is their tagline. But their vision is more comprehensive.

> We the members of the Kingsport mill team will reach safety excellence. To do this we must always demonstrate the highest level of caring, mutual respect, trustworthiness, teamwork, open collaboration to foster ownership and engagement, and positive motivational attitudes. We will rely on, as our foundation, these core processes – standards, policies, work rules, audits, investigations, and follow-up. As a result of reaching safety excellence, we will be sustainable and viable, have a common vision demonstrated with pride and nobody gets hurt.

As we helped them develop their vision we asked what beliefs would support it. We looked at possible factors that could demotivate engagement. We recognized five categories of poor performance: unwilling, unable, unaware, unaccountable, and unlike the culture. We asked what engagement would look like from the perspectives of customers, managers, supervisors, employees, and contractors because **an effective vision directs value-producing behavior**.

What success looks like today will change over time. That could be tomorrow, next month, in three years. This is why you need to keep asking this second performance-improving question: what is the vision? Your vision is based on assumptions. And these are based on what you know. What are your existing assumptions? You've identified your various customers. You've verified what values are important to them. You know what they want. You understand what they need to get the job done. Or do you?

Consider this...

- Can you generate multiple options from which to choose?
- Are you just copying?
- How have previous visions become reality?
- How will your vision be aligned with your culture?
- How will your vision become a reality for everyone?
- How will your vision have the potential to create emotional buy-in? How does your existing organization's vision show up in observable behavior?
- Will your vision be easy to communicate?
- How does vision operate at different levels within the organization?
- Who can you trust to share your new vision with while it's still vulnerable?
- Who can help you determine what your successful vision will look like?

Chapter 7

Rationale

'...important, unimportant, unimportant, important,' as if he
were trying which word sounded best.

— Lewis Carroll, Alice in Wonderland

Question 3: What is the rationale?

At the end of the movie *Annie Hall*, Woody Allen's character, Alvy
Singer, recalls an old joke. A guy goes into the psychiatrist's office
and says, "Doc, my brother's crazy. He thinks he's a chicken." The
doctor replies, "Why don't you turn him in?" The guy says, "I
would, but I need the eggs."[37]

This isn't far removed what happens every day in some
organizations: for example, when career focus comes at the
expense of business effectiveness. Or when short-term self-
interest gets in the way of long-term strategy, you have a
misaligned rationale. The rationale for your visions is simply this:
what makes sense and for whom?

Does your vision make sense?

Your vision tells you what success looks like. Your rationale tests
it and explains how and where you can win. It's based upon
asking the right questions, collecting appropriate data, and
analyzing what it all means. Formulating your rationale is a design
process explaining reasons for embarking on the vision, justifying
it, assessing alternatives, considering tradeoffs, testing expected
value, and identifying effective areas for intervention.

Will your hypothesis work? Is the rationale consistent with your vision? One company's vision was based on the belief that all accidents are preventable. Yet they had a system in place to track non-preventable vehicle accidents. With their vision and rationale misaligned, they were in danger of losing credibility with employees. This mismatch only surfaced as we started to validate their vision.

Are you asking the right questions?

From the 1991 Gulf War until the Iraq War of 2003, the Patriot PAC-2 missile defense system was the only one used in combat by the United States against Iraqi Scud missiles. Official military estimates gave the Patriot approximately a 61 percent success rate (27 successes out of 44 engagements). Investigation by the American Physical Society (APS), a non-profit organization advancing the knowledge of physics, found that the Patriot PAC-2 was a failure.[38] Investigators and the Army were using different criteria for determining success.

Each group was asking different questions. The Army discounted news media video of Patriot-Scud encounters. The APS took into account media footage. The difference of opinion rested upon the **rationale for what success looks like**. For an engagement to be counted as a success by the Army, the rationale had to meet three main criteria: 1) A Scud had to have been launched; 2) At least one Patriot had to intercept the Scud; 3) There must be no significant ground damage or casualties.

Upon further examination, congressional studies showed that 15 percent of the time Patriot missiles were fired at non-existent targets. Thirty percent were fired at only missile debris, not live warheads. "Intercept," as defined by the Army meant firing a missile toward the target. It didn't imply that the target was destroyed. The third criteria meant that lack of *reported* ground damage fulfilled the requirement for success. Both wars were fought in sparsely populated regions.

Your rationale will determine the data you look for. That data will support or sink your initial value-adding hypothesis (the vision), or it may lead you to consider a new and better vision. The rationale is likely to be different depending on the identity and role of your customer. For example, investors want to know why they should invest here and not there. An executive may need to make a case for allocating millions of dollars. Line-employees want to know the reason for redesign of the workplace and expected new behaviors. All stakeholders need explanations. But do these make sense?

A pipeline company was becoming a victim of its own success. It had grown through acquisition to an organization of 15 different entities, each with its own personalities, perspectives, and operational methods. In line with the old adage, 'If it ain't broke, don't fix it,' senior management took a hands-off approach. Yet many of these successful companies were outgrowing their own systems. There was no operational, safety, or customer strategies. They called us in to help them formulate an acquisition strategy for new companies. It started with **questions to determine the rationale**. How will an acquisition add value? How will it fit with existing conditions? What sort of problems will this acquisition generate? Will it distract us from our main purpose?

Will your vision fit?
Is your vision going to be culturally acceptable? Making only a business case without taking into account human feelings is likely to fail. You want to influence hearts and minds before hands and

feet. We were working with a company in the Port of Los Angeles on Terminal Island, California. Our work was to implement a process improvement. The organization had already adopted a Japanese lean manufacturing process: *Kaizen* 5-S. This is a good housekeeping standardization method. If someone wants a wrench, there is an outline drawing on the wall for where it's always kept.

The company wanted to extend what was functioning well into other groups. We planned to add safety (a sixth S) to the process. People who were already following the *Kaizen* 5-S process were doing a good job with it. Our initial rationale was for these people to run the new process with the addition of the new safety "S". We reasoned we could use existing infrastructure for rapid start-up. The team already had internal cohesion. These people had the most experience, so they should lead the effort. But we got pushback. Not everybody's going to get the rationale for everything.

They didn't see our rationale in the beginning. The way they saw it was that no good deed goes unpunished. The analogy was, "We've built a successful harbor, and now you want to come in with your new ship and tie off to us." Since our rationale was generating resistance, we had to create a new process with new people. This wasn't the most efficient system, yet it did work. Your rationale must be culturally acceptable.

The follow-up to this story had a happy ending. We don't believe that engagements between consultants and companies should last forever. About a year later, it was time to cut the umbilical cord. We had a design disengagement point. The new head of the *Kaizen* 5-S initiative sat in on the closeout meeting. He saw a lot of parallel effort and suggested combining teams. This worked well and generated further efficiency and value improvement.

The significant few

What's popular isn't a rationale for what's effective. At a Middle East-based oil company, everyone loved the safety-improvement program. Yet two and a half years into the program, there was a zero return on investment. While it did get people talking to one another, those conversations weren't adding value. We discovered the program had no focus.

A company like this with 15 strategic priorities is not a focused organization. We identified just five safety issues that made a huge improvement. When you can count your priorities on one hand, you have **one-handed strategy.** The Pareto principle states that 80 percent of effects come from 20 percent of causes. So picking the right few has a big impact. Moreover, the Hawthorne Effect comes into play. Individuals modify or improve their behavior in response to being observed.

The most effective way to minimize resistance to change is to minimize the perception of change. Over the next six months, this company improved their performance by doing fewer things and focusing on what mattered most. Eighteen months later, people still believed that they were doing the originally popular program. Even though the name remained the same, the program was radically different. Had we gone in and said, "We're going to change what you're doing," we would've created unnecessary resistance. The rationale for an evolutionary approach helped the customer create new value over time.

Are you confusing cause and correlation?

In Daniel Kahneman's book *Thinking Fast and Slow*, he identifies the illusion of causality when what's really happening are repeated observations of correlation. If you often see two events occurring at the same time, you have the impression one caused the other. Cause is actually *how* one action makes another event happen. What we need to see are structures or behaviors *causing* improvement.

Misuse of correlation is so common among researchers that some statisticians have wished the method had never been devised at all. [39] Confusion between cause and correlation is rife because we are primed from birth to see patterns and draw conclusions. But are they the right ones?

SHAWN: I recently spent a week in a cabin in Minnesota with my in-laws. Most of the people at the gathering were much older than me. The conversation turned to relatives who had passed on. My youngest daughter (seven) was sitting on my lap. She asked me why my goatee had white hair in it. I replied, "Well, Daddy is getting older." My daughter's eyes filled with tears. I said, "What's wrong, honey?" She replied, "I don't want you to die, because people with white hair die." I couldn't help but laugh.

Something good must once have happened to someone who found a four-leaf clover. Somebody else must have had a bad day after a black cat walked across their path. But these events aren't repeatable. Such correlations are misguided attempts at a rationale. All of us need to be aware of a natural impulse to jump to conclusions based on a correlation of too few data points.

Has your vision passed its sell-by date?

How do you determine if your vision continues to be the right one? Your rationale needs constant review. Keep your finger on its pulse. Maintain dialogue. Ask if you're going in the right direction. Continually monitor performance and value. Know your rationale for any behavior change. What's your rationale to stop doing something? A clear understanding of the "why" is the first step to be able to communicate it. You're not just measuring activities and results. Look to create value, change beliefs, and change knowledge. Keep asking: Is this vision still relevant?

Organizations monitor their outside strategies through customer surveys and marketing research. Inside strategies also need to be constantly aligned and realigned with the voice of the customer. Ask your workers if the strategy works, makes sense, and helps them make right decisions.

When formulating your rationale, there's always the problem of what to leave out. Reasons may be complex, involving multidimensional factors of hard and soft costs, fluctuations in business conditions, and perceptual changes. But the factors that hold **meaning** for stakeholders will be the ones they remember. This challenges you to engage emotions and answer their question: **what's in it for me?**

If you're going to make your rationale stick, you need to tell a story.

Consider this...

- Why is your vision relevant?
- Which data is informing you?
- Is your rationale based on a business case alone?
- How will you engage hearts and minds?

- What might change to make your vision irrelevant?
- Why will your vision get buy-in?
- Will your vision make sense within your culture?
- Are you asking the right questions? How do you know?
- How does your vision minimize resistance?
- How are you avoiding mixing up cause and correlation?

Chapter 8
Story

Stories are the single most powerful weapon in a leader's arsenal.

—Howard Gardner, professor and author

Question 4: What is the story?

At a quality convention, a senior executive related a story of how a manufacturing division had struggled with quality issues. He told of their efforts over the past three years to understand and solve the root causes of their defects. He went on to say how, for the first time, the division had achieved six-sigma quality.

Everyone cheered.

Then, in a quiet voice, he asked, "But how important do you think this story is to the six people who found our products didn't work right out of the box?" As you probably guessed, this story was a boost for the manufacturing division, but it didn't mean much to those few customers who had received poor products the previous month. Your story has to fit its audience. Stories make ideas stick.

Stories in the form of parables, myths, allegories, and fables have communicated ideas, expectations, and reasons since the dawn of time. Stories explain, influence and persuade. And they do that by engaging the listener's imagination. You see a story unfold in your minds' eye. A persuasive story talks to your head and heart.

Effective business stories have a beginning, middle, and end. Such stories need tension and struggle. Initially there's a problem, and by twists and (often wrong) turns the problem gets resolved. There is one more thing an effective story needs, and we'll get to that in just a moment. But before we do, let's look at this three-part structure.

In the above story, the beginning was the manufacturing division's problem of quality. In the middle of the story it struggled for three years. In the end, it achieved six-sigma status. And so the story is resolved. But this particular story opens the door to a new problem and a new story to be told; namely, there is more work to do. While quality has improved, it hasn't been improved for everyone—yet!

Getting your story right is a high-stakes proposition. Stories have purpose. They can inspire individuals to great success, or in the case of enemy propaganda, seek to instill a sense of futility and inevitability. Stories can also clarify ideas and expectations. They can make a rationale or complex ideas understandable by showing concrete examples.

An executive confided in us that his team was committed to executing their aggressive strategy. They had created the vision. They understood the rationale. Yet they were less confident about how to communicate it to inspire action. They needed a story.

As we showed in Chapter 4, consultant and educator Ruby Payne taught us how different groups process information. This important point is often overlooked. Her work showed a tendency in some groups to learn from specific to general, whereas most teaching is the opposite, from abstract to concrete. Stories need to be relevant and coherent. Internal strategy uses stories for every level, every team, and every individual in your organization. You need a story, but expect to have more than one version of it.

One senior executive, addressing his employees, expressed his exemplary reason for change. He began, "When I was three years old, my grandfather lost his life in an industrial accident. I never had the opportunity to learn from him and I want to make sure your grandchildren, one day, have the opportunity to learn from you. This is why what we are doing in safety is so important." Then he went on to make the business case. Yet what people remember is what matters to them personally, their own families. Your story needs **emotional connection,** at the same time expressing why it adds value to participating individuals. When communication focuses solely on a rationale for business, it fails to convince the hearts of listeners. A meaningful personal and emotional rationale for change sticks.

Your story must speak to your listeners in a way they can understand. Tell it in multiple ways for different constituents. How can you express your vision and rationale quickly, clearly, and to the point? If you think this sounds like an elevator pitch, you'd be right. Rumor has it that the thirty-second presentation came about in the early days of Hollywood. Screenwriters would hope to catch the top floor executives in the elevator and use that brief ride to pitch their movie idea. The elevator pitch evolved to become a standard tactic of sales training and networking. It's now a tool for inside strategy.

Takeaway

So, we described the simple three-part story structure, but we have not yet addressed a missing vital element of a business story: the takeaway. First, let's tell a story.

TERRY: I was presenting at a convention. I couldn't help but notice the well-dressed man in the front row paying particular attention and taking notes. After my talk, he approached me and without even saying hello asked if we could meet. He was the president of a large company and told me that his people would sort out the details. He did say that his organization, with an excellent safety record, had recently had an increase in accidents. Not long afterward, we signed a contract to help them.

After some analysis, we identified four critical behaviors that would positively impact approximately 83 percent of his accidents. These four behaviors had to be memorable. The company reinforced the new behavior message in their monthly newsletter. Their next seven projects went without a hitch. Then accidents started to occur again. I got a call to go and find out what was happening. I discovered two more behaviors that had not been in our original four. The company was experiencing traffic accidents in rural Kansas. There are no stop signs in such a sparsely populated area. Visibility is restricted because of cornfields. The company's response was for employees to take the National Safety Council distracted driver training. I visited this training and waited outside as people came out of the class. I asked them, "What are the three types of distracted driving?" Not a single person could name all three. Takeaway failed.

Despite the fact that people had been exposed to information just minutes before, it hadn't sunk in. They needed a story. So our takeaway became, "If you want to be a safe driver, you need to be an ACE." When you think of ACE, what comes to mind? The answer will be different for each individual. Some will think of a champion, others might think of a playing card. In this instance, ACE stood for Attention, Control, and Eyes on the road. We built this sequence of events back into the National Safety Council's program. We relabeled parts of the program to make them this sticky acronym. We were rewarded by fabulous results. This one-line takeaway focused behavior.

We continue to support and reinforce inside strategy though easy-to-remember takeaways. Acronyms help remind people what to do. Stories tell them why they are doing it. What do you remember from the above story? The well-dressed man? ACE? What people take away from a story depends on each individual.

Better story, better results

How do people see themselves as actors in the story? In Chapter 7, we explained how Domtar Corporation in their paper and pulp business created teams, each with their own special mission to keep people safe. S.E.A.L. (Safety, Excellence, Awareness, and Leadership) teams have graphics and insignia similar to elite Special Forces. This internal branding effort creates a coherent and consistent narrative so teams and their members take on specific identities. Names of teams lean on a strong military metaphor. For example, Team Eagle signifies mastery, excellence and guidance. Team Recon is represented by the symbol of a bugle which connotes leading through communication and keeping each other informed. Domtar has an outstanding safety record.

Domtar understands the power of story to turn abstract ideas into real events. Workers recount their real-world stories in videos which are uploaded to the company's website. Effective strategic stories give people **a sense of belonging**. It shows them where they fit and how they add value. Perhaps even more important, a successful story **conveys meaning**.

Our experience shows that **those who communicate better, perform better**. Culture is made of common beliefs and values. Your story has to fit each culture. Simply imposing a story without understanding the emotional investment people have already made is asking for resistance. We've come to the conclusion that people don't resist change. They change all the time. It's being changed by force that they resist. John Kotter, a management consultant, author, and Harvard business professor, writes that people respond emotionally to change before they respond logically. Kotter identifies three triggers to resisting change. First, people don't understand the change. This is a communication problem. Second, people don't like the change. They don't see what's in it for them. Third, they don't like who is bringing the change. What matters is credibility and trust.

A story tells us who we are, what we believe, what we value, and what we are trying to do. Since ancient times, stories have been a powerful method of igniting the imagination and giving people a reason to believe. It's far more effective to change beliefs than to try to change behaviors. Today, successful organizations are paying more attention to the stories they tell. Stories are a natural communication method. When people socialize, they tell each other stories of what's meaningful to them. Your story focuses attention and promotes beliefs, values, and behaviors to shape the future you want.

Consider this...
- Do you have a story or stories?

- Is your story still relevant?
- Are you telling the right stories?
- Are they understandable?
- Do they fit with the culture?
- What effect are you seeing from the stories you tell?
- How do new beliefs inspired by stories change behavior?
- Can people identify with the story?
- Can they see themselves as actors in it?
- How much investment will you make to communicate your story?

Now that you've identified your customer, created your rationale, and packaged it into a story, it's time to look at boundaries and our next question: what is the scope?

Chapter 9
Boundaries

The difference between stupidity and genius is that genius has its limits.
—Albert Einstein, physicist

Question 5: What is the scope?

During World War II, the first objective for the allied invasion of Normandy was to establish a beachhead. Once secured, it became a landing ground for men and equipment. Only then could the allies press further into occupied territory. Establishing a beachhead is a function of scope. Starting small allows you to focus your attention. You can expand your boundaries later.

Strategic scope can also be linear, a series of battles that will gain ground, consolidate position, and ultimately win the war. What's important is to judge your ability to implement and sustain your effort. Quick wins build confidence; early failures make second tries more difficult.

Expectations
Defining the scope aligns expectations. There are still important questions to be asked before you choose what to do and how you're going to support long-term performance improvement. Let's look at the strategic thinking you've already done. You know your purpose. You've identified your customers. You know what they value. You've formulated a vision and done some thinking about your rationale. And you've created a possible story. Now it's time to think about the extent of what you want to accomplish. Where should your focus be? How small or large is

your initial undertaking? You don't have answers yet, but you do need to make some educated guesses. What we know is that small strategic victories build confidence.

Scope is a boundary. It defines the extent of your expectations and commitment of resources, time, and costs. Identifying the scope doesn't mean coming to complete decisions. We are still in hypothesis country, unless you already have data which will tell you what your choices need to be. Occasionally people contact us wanting answers to cost and scope before even asking the questions. But prescription before diagnosis is bad medicine.

Scope focuses attention

Michael Menard, co-founder of the GenSight Group and author of a book on project portfolio management,[40] identifies a practice he calls "singing for their lunch" where senior managers optimistically oversell their own project ideas, minimizing scope, costs, and time to completion. Who wins here is often the person with the best story and the least painful offer. Menard says the antidote to blind optimism is to put feedback systems in place so ideas can be measured against actuality. Advocates then take a more thoughtful and realistic approach about what they are championing.

By establishing boundaries you can avoid "scope creep." That is, doing more than agreed upon. Scope summarizes the extent of what is to be done.

Correcting course

Your original idea is likely to undergo change as you gather data. You're testing your narrative. This is not a pass/fail test. Inside strategy's ten-question framework is an iterative process. New information helps you correct course. You may need to go back and reexamine your previous assumptions. As you start making decisions, anticipate modifying your expectations.

What was relevant yesterday may not be appropriate today. Maybe experience or data shows you are not going to accomplish your complete objective in year one. Usually you'll need to revise the scope in light of what you discover. Maybe there's more you need to do, or more you need to undo.

As the famous Mike Tyson quote says, "Everyone has a plan until they get punched in the mouth."[41] The trouble with unforeseen circumstances is they're invisible, until they're not. What's unknown today is likely to make itself known tomorrow. Whatever the scope, it's probably going to take longer to achieve than you hoped it would. In subsequent chapters we'll examine what the data is telling us about choosing initiatives and priorities.

Time boundaries can be inflexible. We worked with an organization that had 300+ locations around the world. They wanted to implement a change methodology over a three-year period at all 300 locations. Typically a boots-on-the-ground single lead consultant requires an engagement of about 20 days over a 12-month period. We realized, understanding the scope presented to us, this wasn't something we could lead internally.

We took a hybrid approach. We identified key internal personnel and coached them to become internal consultants to implement the process. Along the way, the unknowns started to become known. The company experienced employee attrition. Some locations had production issues causing them to stall. Other sites had to be idled for a time because of interruption in the supply chain. Problems surfaced that were outside the control of the corporation. Even to the best of our ability, we implemented the change in only about 70 percent of the sites during that time. We had a well-defined scope, but time limits, complexity, and size of change meant that the scope was more guesswork than we would have liked it to be.

Another time, we were engaged by a large consumer product company. Part of the company's process improvement initiative called for each business unit to maintain a behavioral checklist. Policy required sites to annually change focus on specific behaviors. We asked them why. Avoiding monotony was their reasoning. So, we asked, what if data tells you you're already focusing on what's relevant. A change from relevant scope causes your focus to be shifted *away* from what matters most. Change of focus needs to come from what the system is telling you, not some blanket policy. Revisiting your scope is essential. Are you still focusing on the right things? But beware of your reasoning. Data (if you have it) should determine the scope. If you don't yet have data, you're back to your best hypothesis, the educated guess.

Transformational thinking

Learning changes anatomy. We grow brain cells in response to new challenge. The body responds to demand, which is why tennis players practice their strokes and dancers drill their steps. Train with weights and you actually tear muscles in order for them to repair to a stronger state. The nineteenth century philosopher Fredrick Nietzsche wrote, "That which does not kill us, makes us stronger." This may be going too far, but you get the idea. The human system responds to change, and anatomical growth takes time. Cognitive abilities change in response to environment and demand. Too much too soon creates overwhelm. This is the reason to start small and monitor what happens.

Performance improvement is both physical and cognitive. For decades the idea that a single neuron fires in response to a concept was dismissed by the scientific community. However, over the last ten years or so, this notion has undergone further study. John Medina's book *Brain Rules* explains how fans who like to watch reruns of the sitcom *Friends* will have a "Jennifer Aniston neuron." The neuron fires in response to something you see often. Scientists now believe that some types of memory formation are linked to object-specific neurons.[42] You see what looks to you like a familiar configuration and your brain responds with a habitual pattern. Shifting these responses is at the heart of transformational thinking.

There are no perfect formulas for developing scope. Can people cognitively or physically expand their capabilities? If data tells us yes, we can, this is usually what happens over time. Which few behaviors might produce the best results? As you start to make small changes, data comes back to you. Now you can revisit the scope in light of what you've learned.

Consider this... How well have your defined your scope? Is it in writing?

- What size of change are you looking at? Is it the right size? Why is that?
- What one thing can you do to make the biggest positive impact?
- What small change do you want to see?

- How are you making room for contingencies? Are you seriously taking unknowns into consideration or are you hoping for the best?
- Where are the scope boundaries and how will you contain them?
- How will you determine the scope? Do you have data? Is your guess educated enough or do you need to go back to previous stages?
- What are your initial expectations? Why are they realistic? What has to happen? What has to not happen?
- What biases are active?
- What are the cost boundaries? How flexible are they? Are costs aligned with expected value?
- What does commitment look like? Who will do what by when?
- Who are the dissenters? Do they have well-argued positions? Could they be right?
- Where are the hearts and minds right now?
- Are you trying to do too much?
- Are you able to focus on the agreed-upon scope? What might distract you?
- How will you handle distractions?
- What will you **not** do to make room for additional effort?
- If you initially create your beachhead, how will you then expand the scope?
- If you don't initially succeed what will you do next?
- Is there evidence of transformational thinking? What does that look like?

We'll now go into our sixth strategic performance improving question: What supports or conflicts with your ability to succeed?

Chapter 10
Snipers or support?

First we shape our dwellings, and then they shape us.
—Winston Churchill, British statesman

Question 6: What supports or conflicts with your ability to succeed?

Shawn: Is your culture going to work with you? My experience in the military taught me it's a bad idea to get surprised by sniper fire. You want to be prepared. You have to identify where danger lies before it gets you. You need to minimize the possibility of being ambushed. And this analogy works within the organization. What do conditions on the ground look like? Are you going to be shot at by snipers or supported in your strategic purpose?

Aristotle wrote that man is by nature a political animal.[43] This is as true today as it was thousands of years ago. Politics is a reality in any organization. As we wrote in the introduction, data will influence your decision to move forward with your strategy or step back and reevaluate. But will the data you discover or generate (See Chapter 11: Digging for data) be acceptable as evidence for change? Or will you be ambushed by entrenched belief systems that will reject your findings? Culture determines beliefs and behaviors, so it makes sense to pay attention to existing political realities because these will tell you what's possible and what isn't.

What is your culture telling you?

Take the case of a global manufacturer that hired us to help them put in place a safety management system. The factory in question was in a resource-challenged country. Global safety policy stipulated mandatory wearing of company-provided, steel-toed shoes. But an early challenge was getting these people to wear appropriate clothing. It wasn't long before management noticed people weren't complying. People would switch out their steel-toed shoes for home sandals. Managers discovered that wearing shoes to work wasn't a cultural norm. The organization hadn't been listening so it wasn't aware of existing norms. It was trying to impose a policy on a culture that didn't support it.

Observations can tell you a lot about a culture. A caustic 2015 investigative New York Times article[44] describes the Darwinian work culture at Amazon. According to the article, employees are pitted against each other, and working hours are extreme. Rules dominate. Confrontation is the norm. New employees are required to pay back part of their signing bonus if they leave within a year. Attrition is high. The same article states that in 2011, a newspaper investigation uncovered Amazon's practice of having workers toiling in 100 degree heat while ambulances waited outside the facility to take away the fallen. Only after the situation became public did Amazon install air conditioning.

While Amazon's culture is an example of "Digital Taylorism,"[45] Oscar Munoz, United Airlines' new CEO, is setting out to improve employee and customer morale. He admits there's a culture problem. And in United's case, it results in poor customer and employee experience. Previous to Munoz's leadership, the company's goal of record profits got in the way of strategic sustainability.[46] In his open letter to all employees, he shows he understands what's important to them. He recognizes their frustrations, admits there's a problem, and plans to address it. One of his first acts is to listen.

Buy-in

New ideas are vulnerable to being shot down for many reasons, one of which is because you thought of them and your critics didn't. John Kotter and Lorne Whitehead[47] write that 70 percent of the time when significant large-scale change is called for, people don't follow through with support. Instead they go into denial, leave, actually try to fail, or quit halfway through the project using twice the resources in terms of time and money. While Kotter and Whitehead are making the case, rightly, for incremental change, an important focus of attention needs to be on cultivating ongoing support.

We know your strategic vision makes sense to you, but does it make sense to other people? You still have to sell your idea. As you bring ideas to your customers, you need to understand what's in it for them. And to understand that, you have to ask. Maybe men are socially conditioned not to ask for driving directions. But both men and women can ask for information in a way that doesn't compromise credibility. Mindreading is risky. It's better to ask. You need to know what people value, and how it will help the organization. And, just as important, how will it help people as individuals?

This is where personal relationships matter. It isn't enough to guess what your customers value. Apart from being a winning leadership trait, genuine curiosity about other people is a source of relevant information. In order for something to be a good idea, you have to shape the experiences that will shape beliefs. You can't force an epiphany. You can't force somebody to believe something. But you can build relationships and experiences that will shape beliefs over time.

Be specific

Show what adequate support looks like. Who will commit to what? How will people benefit? In a top-down organization, decision making can be rapid. Your task is to get agreement among decision makers in this complex environment. What would have to be true for an idea to gain traction?

Beware of pitfalls. Everybody's competing for resources at higher levels in organizations. Emotions can run high as people promote their agendas. How can you minimize the pain of change, or the perception of it? Starting small reduces contingencies.

The old adage, "actions speak louder than words," is true. What does leadership behavior tell you? Can you identify unstated goals? Are words and deeds aligned? If things don't pan out this time, what will you do? Then there are the unknowns you can't plan for, and this is where strategic thinking comes into its own.

Use what you have

Remember Helmuth von Moltke's essential strategic idea of doing more with what you already have? We were engaged by a chemical company. They used a great sales-driven coaching model with customers. Just about everybody in a leadership position had been trained to use this model.

We realized the methodology was sound and could be used to coach people toward performance improvement. Using these existing techniques minimized the perception of change. Our intervention met with no resistance because no one saw it as an imposition from outside. It made sense. Consider what making sense means. It's familiar and fits within the existing framework. We avoided the "here-comes-more-*#@!!-training!" This was evolution instead of revolution. Our strategy leveraged what we already knew and found a new focus for it.

Why copying doesn't work

The urge to copy is instinctual. A very long time ago, people figured out that eating one type of plant gave them energy, and another type caused them to fall down and never get up again. Observation and copying is how we survived as humans. Instinct does have a place in strategic thinking, but it's tempered by rationality.

As we said at the beginning of this book, rigid planning fails when circumstances change. Your original idea is likely to undergo change as you gather data and uncover new beliefs and values. According to what might be legend, on the eve of the Battle of Waterloo in 1815, Lord Uxbridge, commander of the cavalry and second-in-command, came to the Duke of Wellington and asked what he should do if Wellington was killed in battle. Pointing toward the enemy, Wellington replied, "That depends upon what he is going to do." Wellington was referring to Napoleon. Strategy requires modifying your plan to fit circumstances. This is why simply trying to copy someone else's plan can lead you to a place you don't want to go.

Imposing a system without regard to culture is an act of violence. The internet is crammed with free advice for best practices. If they're new to you, these tips may be useful. But they can rarely be used literally. Are they appropriate for your circumstances? Because some successful people get up each morning and run five miles before breakfast doesn't mean that if you do the same, you'll be just as successful.

We authors are about 5 feet 8 inches tall. We'll never play for the NBA. But there are other things we can be good at. Take lean manufacturing as an example. It's talked about less these days. Although it has sound principles, the main reason it hasn't been successful is incompatibility with cultures trying to adopt it. New directions and capabilities must become part of the DNA of the culture. In the 1980s, American companies were falling over themselves to emulate Japanese success. But the two cultures are radically different. Can we learn from other cultures? Yes. Should we copy them? No.

Globalization has forced us to be more culturally aware. Even if organizations are based in the United States, customers are more likely to be in other parts of the world. Preferences differ by culture. According to a survey,[48] people preferred toothpaste with the least amount of artificial ingredients in India, France, and Brazil, whereas in the United States, convenience and taste mattered most. Cultures differ by country, but cultural preferences differ by organization and sub-cultures within a company. People don't wear suits and ties at Apple. Group pressure to conform is strong. What are the pressures in your organization, and how will this impact your strategy?

Can your culture carry out your strategies? For example, how accepting of risk is your culture? Getting out of bed is risky. But so is staying in bed. Every action is subject to risk. What do you view as an acceptable risk? What do you view as an unacceptable risk? Why? Is the scope acceptable? Experts say it's easier to demotivate people than motivate them. What existing factors might be demotivating? You may need to go back and reexamine existing beliefs and values. Consider how decisions are made within your organization. Does leadership exhibit foresight and flexibility? Or does change only come when things get too painful, or when the cost of doing nothing is greater than doing something new? Look at which capabilities currently exist. Leverage those so they generate new value.

Not any more

People believed cigarettes were good for you because a man in a white coat on TV said so. Now advertisements for physician-recommended cigarettes are thankfully things of the past. Over time, cultural norms are modified and change. Employees leave or retire, new ones are hired. New memes replicate throughout an organization. Business conditions change. Economic cycles fluctuate. In a wider context, social attitudes are constantly shifting. During the Industrial Revolution, safe drinking water wasn't widely available. Workers drank beer in factories. You can imagine the safety issues. Until recently, smoking in the workplace was the norm. Now it's forbidden. For decades, power companies turned a blind eye to employees hopping a fence to read the meter. Clearly no employee wants to be confronted with a vicious dog, or a shotgun-wielding angry customer. There've been many injuries due to fence-hopping. Today, with use of automatic meter readers, this dangerous practice has fallen away. Attitudes and practices take time to change.

People respond emotionally to change before they do logically.
As we discussed in the previous chapter, none of us is free from bias. Here is a thought experiment. You support political party A. You dislike political party B. The candidate you support makes a mistake and gets hammered by the opposition. Is your first instinct defense? Do you think anyone could make such a mistake? Do you think the mistake isn't relevant? Or are you likely to agree with the opposition? Now reverse the situation.

The candidate you dislike makes the same mistake. Are you likely to think that's typical and they were rotten to the core anyway? Or would you give them the benefit of the doubt? Only you know the answers. Strong emotions have a habit of blotting out rational thinking. But, of course, you need to engage hearts *and* minds.

What supports or conflicts with your ability to succeed? This is now the central question in your strategic process. Being in the right place at the right time rarely happens by chance. More often, it's a result of strategic thinking. And being in the right place at the right time is well out of the way of sniper fire.

Consider this...

- Who are the influencers?
- Who are you ignoring?
- How will you minimize resistance?
- Do goals get in the way of performance improvement? How?
- What's undiscussable (the proverbial elephant in the room)?
- What do people have difficulty understanding? Why?
- What gets hidden and why?
- What cultural/organizational antagonisms exist?
- What cultural/organizational synergies are present?
- How are sub-goals dependent upon each other?
- What are the political realities? How will you test for them?
- How will you manage what you can't change?

Chapter 11
Digging for data

In God we trust. All others must bring data.
—W. Edwards, author and consultant

Question 7: What data-driven priorities and objectives would be of strategic value?

You know what success looks like. You've identified your customers. You've specified the value you want to deliver to them. You've determined the rationale, story, and scope. You've examined what supports or conflicts with your ability to succeed. You've gained buy-in to go further. Now is the time for exploration, to look at the data you have and what you need to generate. This is an iterative four-part process.

1. Decide which data you need.
2. Conduct your search.
3. Interpret your findings.
4. Put in place a small intervention and monitor what happens.

Decide

How you frame your story will tell you what type of data you need. Your data will suggest which path to take. You need to see what's relevant. We all swim in data. Yet, more information doesn't mean we are better informed. The opposite may be true. Data overload can be stupefying. Narrowing your options may be a better choice.

Big data just keeps getting bigger. Big data allows for vast numbers to be visualized and crunched into finer and finer detail. We know a lot more about a wide range of topics. But this doesn't necessarily make choosing among options easier. Which data is going to be most useful to improve performance? Which data will tell you how acceptable your proposed intervention will be? What data exists about beliefs, values, and behaviors?

The signal we are looking for can be lost in the noise. And this is the challenge. More choices can overwhelm the human mind to the extent that choosing not to choose becomes the default choice. As you go through your decision-making process, think about things you can take off the table. Limiting choice is effective, but the difficult question is: how will you narrow your options? How will you decide? This is a task for a human.

What are you going to look for? What will you measure? Your organization may have a formal decision-making process. What do you already know? Can that methodology be leveraged here? Are those things you already measure leading to insight? There will always be constraints because your culture has to be able to absorb your intervention. You want improvement but you don't want to rock the boat so much that it sinks. This is why you're looking for data that will allow you to make small changes that will have a big effect. You want data upon which you can act.

What will be most effective? Why? Is your accessible data useful? What are indicators telling you?

We identify three types of indicators: lagging, leading, and transformational. Consider your health. Having a heart attack (or not having one) is a **lagging indicator**: a measure of a past result. A **leading indicator** measures your activity. For example, one measure of the effectiveness of your exercise program is calories burned versus calories consumed. Let's assume you achieve measurable results and you're burning more calories and consuming fewer. Is this a good thing? At first glance, you'd think so. But what if all this exercise and diet is sending your blood pressure up to dangerous levels? Should you exercise more? Should you keep restricting your food intake? No, more of the same is unlikely to be the sensible answer. Your blood pressure is telling you that you need a different intervention. This is a **transformational indicator**. It measures the value derived from your activities.

When it comes to performance improvement, lagging indicators don't tell you enough. They tell you what has happened. The trouble is what happened in the past may—or may not—have much to do with future behavior. Consider the last two British Petroleum (BP) accidents. In March of 2005 a hydrocarbon vapor cloud exploded at BP's Texas City's refinery killing 15 people and injuring 100. Five years later, an explosion sunk the Deepwater Horizon oil rig in the Gulf of Mexico causing loss of life, injury, and an environmental disaster. Ironically, just days before each catastrophe, leadership had given out awards for safety performance.

Results are consequences of behavior. This doesn't mean you should ignore lagging indicators. You need to know precisely how you got to where you are today. Lagging indicators can be a benchmark from which to measure current and future performance. The problem with benchmarks is using the wrong bench. And only focusing on results can lead to false confidence.

Leading indicators measure activities.

Just because you wake up at dawn doesn't mean your awakening caused the sun to rise. False confidence happens when you misattribute cause. You can measure how many people are enrolled in ongoing education, but it doesn't tell you anything about their contribution to value. Cause isn't something you can assume. There's a word for belief in an unexamined cause: superstition. Baseball has a long history of superstition. Some players believe that bathing after a win will lead to subsequent failure. Just because you perform a pre-game ritual and you win doesn't mean that specific activity caused the result. And less superstition makes for a better-smelling workplace.

Transformational indicators measure value between activities and results.

Transformational indicators measure the value of activities. For example, does training change what people believe and know? Does it change behavior? In Chapter 8, we described how not a single person who had just participated in a distracted driver training could name all three types of distracted driving. Checking the training attendance box only tells you so much. It's not a given that such training is going to transform behavior. Transformational indicators look for change in people's behaviors, capabilities, and contribution to value. They measure visible progress, thus narrowing your focus.

Find

We've helped many organizations narrow their focus. From a safety perspective, we want to know what kinds of accidents happen most often. We may or may not have accident data. We ask employees what they think is the accident most likely to happen to them. We aren't looking for severity of incidents, but frequency of accidents. We see then if respondent perceptions match a Pareto analysis of their accident data—mostly they don't. Focusing workers on the most common types of accidents can make their safety efforts more effective.

Knowing what you're looking for is essential. A construction company identified several vital characteristics of leadership behavior. In their leadership development effort, we conducted a search to gather data that would tell us whether people in leadership positions actually embodied these traits. This is not a one-time project. Companies need ongoing leadership development. In our experience, 60 percent of organizations see continual leadership improvement as a top priority.

In 1928, Alexander Fleming discovered penicillin, but not because he was looking for it. He'd forgotten to sterilize bacteria left on plates by an open window while he went off on vacation. When he returned he noticed a mold where no bacteria were growing. If he hadn't been alert to this, and taken appropriate action, hundreds of thousands of lives would not have been saved. Know what you're looking for, but notice what else might be of value.

So many advances in science came about by simply noticing. Data isn't just quantitative, it's qualitative, too. Observing attitudes and behavior can indicate likely acceptance or rejection of your change hypothesis. Reading between the lines can be informative as you listen as much to what people don't say as to what they do say.

Social pressure influences responses. Rather than give an honest opinion when answering questions, people will often reply according to how they think they should respond. An Ernst & Young survey showed that 65 percent of college students polled about their futures thought they would become millionaires.[49]

Polls are an easy way to influence responses and get the answers you want through leading questions. Uninformed respondents are easily manipulated. Beware of how you ask questions. Are they leading or neutral? Remember: you're looking for insight to disprove your hypothesis or find evidence to support it.

Interpret

Interpreting data isn't easy. You need a programmer to debug a software application. You need a physician to interpret an MRI. And to complicate matters, two doctors may disagree on the meaning of the same data. Judgment is human. Who has the right capability to actually interpret what you're seeing?

It's easy to fall into the trap of drawing wrong conclusions from data. This is where critical thinking is of utmost importance. According to research cited by author and columnist David Brooks,[50] in 1966, 19 percent of high school students graduated with an A or A-. Yet by 2013, a survey by UCLA found that 53 percent of high school students graduated with an A or A-.

What does this mean? Have students become more hardworking and intelligent? Or, has high school become less demanding? Like the children in fictional Lake Wobegon, MN, are *all* the children above average? What other factors could be responsible for this data? The numbers alone don't tell us. But these figures do suggest further lines of productive inquiry.

Misinterpreting data can lead to a false sense of confidence. There's data you think you can use, but it's really useless. We conducted a perception survey at one company. Initially we were pleased that employees believed they were getting what they thought was the right information from incident reports. However, it didn't take long to discover their data wasn't deep enough. These reports only identified the injuries. For example, "hurt right shoulder." There was nothing about the conditions that may have caused such an injury. This data was useless as an aid to prevent future occurrences.

Does your data really support how you can create value? Are patterns you think you identify really there? Do you have enough data points? How will your findings be of specific use?

See what happens

Data influences behavior. Giving people data can boost confidence to improve performance. In one study,[51] village students in northern India were given average test scores for all children in school. They were also given their own report cards so they could compare themselves with the average. A year later, school attendance in participating villages had improved, along with increased proficiency in mathematics, English, and Urdu. The villagers could now see what was possible. This simple intervention was cheap and effective. Value resides in strategic thinking and choosing which intervention to try.

According to an article in the journal *Science*, some 1.2 billion people around the globe attempt to survive on less than $1.25 USD per day. A group of researchers have implemented short- and long-term interventions in an attempt to improve the lot of these people.[52] But programs thought to work, in fact don't. For example, microloans are helpful, but not sufficient by themselves to raise people from poverty. In some poor countries, organizations encourage educational participation through scholarships. Yet a simple intervention in Kenya of giving children anti-parasite pills proved to be 51 times as cost-effective as scholarships.

Anti-parasite pills keep children healthy enough to go to school, and so gain knowledge, which gives them a better economic chance. Researchers[53] tracked children into adulthood who received anti-parasite pills. They found that these anti-parasite pill recipients' adult wages were 20 percent higher than people who didn't get the pills in childhood. Ninety-five million children have now received the pills in India and sub-Saharan Africa. Effective interventions don't have to be expensive to implement, but they do need to be well thought-out.

An organization in Charleston, South Carolina, prioritized system-wide risk reduction. Scope encompassed everything from business to employee risk. They had numerous insight-gathering processes in place. At a management meeting, we saw data that showed us most risky behavior happened at lunchtime. The first impulse could have been uninformed intervention, but pausing proved to be the wiser course of action. We needed to know more, so we could narrow focus and decide which interventions would be appropriate.

The plant manager allocated a few employees to make observations at lunchtime and report back. The observers saw people rushing. They saw people taking shortcuts by climbing on the sides of machinery. But the most interesting thing they saw was people wrapping their food in tinfoil and placing it on the steam pipes. Why would people do this?

Observers discovered there was only one microwave in the lunch room for about forty people taking their lunch break at the same time. The problem was structural, forcing people to innovate. Not wanting to find fault with employees, the plant manager didn't say anything. He just bought more microwaves. Over the next few months he continued to monitor at lunchtime. Risks had decreased. If you don't know why you have risk, you don't know how to fix it. Searching for the right data made the right intervention possible.

Be relevant. You want news you can use.

Consider this...

- Which data do you want?
- What data is available?
- How easy is it to access?
- Is it understandable?
- What information will you need to generate?
- What capabilities currently exist?
- Which capabilities could reasonably be learned?
- Are your research questions designed to confirm your pre-formed opinion?
- How are you avoiding leading questions?
- Which biases might skew what you look for?
- Who will interpret your data?
- What expertise or insight is needed to interpret your data?
- Why will the data you hope to find be relevant?
- What do operational performance indicators tell you?
- What will the data allow you to do?

Chapter 12
Choosing

Forgiveness means giving up all hope of a better past.
—Lily Tomlin, actor and comedian

Question 8: Which initiatives will best support your objectives?

Dr. Larry Brilliant's 2006 TED talk[54] proposed that the way to eradicate diseases in the world is through what he calls "early detection, early response." When choosing a strategic intervention, it makes sense to look for one that will have a small input but a large beneficial output. **What strategic intervention will have the most effect, be easiest to implement, and at the same time, be aligned with your strategic goals, and your company and customer values?** We'll address the question of creating alignment in the next chapter. For now, our focus is on making a relevant choice.

If you want different results, you have to make a choice to do something—or stop doing something. Either way, choosing is an active decision because even not choosing is a choice. As we saw in the last chapter, data should inform your decision. But data alone will not make the decision for you. You have to take into consideration how well your approach is likely to be supported. How well will it fit with your existing processes? What's important here is to consider your choice in the light of cultural acceptability. So, if you have prospective interventions that clearly won't play nicely with your culture, then reconsider them.

118

Choosing narrows future options, and then eliminates all but a few. Choose wisely.

Quick wins

The earlier you can show value, the better. In his book about American military command,[55] Thomas E. Ricks points out that the essence of generalship is what you do before the fighting begins. When making your choice, look for **easy wins and widespread visibility.** How will the decision you make support your vision of success? How will you monitor value and its perception?

As we said earlier, visible progress builds confidence. This is why starting small by picking the low-hanging fruit can disarm naysayers. And there will be skeptics. As the saying goes, "Keep your friends close, but your enemies closer." Remember to engage those people likely to resist your business improvement objective because **people support what they help to create.** What expertise will help you make a sound choice? Which teams, committees, and other groups will have political influence on the outcome of your choice? What can they tell you that you don't already know?

Right speed

Are you spending enough time and resources on making your choice?

Earlier in this book, we talked about memes, those sticky ideas that spread through organizations. They often go unexamined and unchallenged. Asking the question "why" gives you pause for thought. Speed and action are common memes that can spread beyond their effective boundaries. For example, John Kotter rightly advocates for a sense of urgency. This is effective inside the boundary of when you know exactly what you're doing or when you must act quickly within a window of opportunity. Faster may usually be better, but not in all contexts.

To paraphrase Paracelsus, a Renaissance-era toxicologist, the right amount of medicine cures, too much kills. This is equally true of speed and efficiency. Urgency is fine in the right context, but can be harmful in the wrong one. In the military, they teach you how to fire a weapon: breathe, relax, aim, squeeze. It's not aim, fire. When you're spending more time aiming, you demonstrate maturity of long-term thinking rather than going in with guns blazing. Results take time despite the impulse for instant gratification. Underestimating how long it will take for a decision to yield results is a common failing. Keep the long-term perspective in mind even though you're looking for quick wins.

There's a right speed for everything. But where the urgency meme is out of control, we see an impulse for people to jump right in with a solution without due consideration. That solution is often a cookie cutter program instead of doing the hard work of strategic thinking. All too often, rushing to action can take the place of consideration and skip necessary steps, or take shortcuts to the detriment of the project.

British comedian Peter Cook once said in an interview that he had learned from his mistakes. He learned so well he could repeat every one of them. Unlike Cook, leaders don't want to fall into the same traps they were caught by in the past. What one culture sees as hesitation, another sees as care.

Expect to be wrong
If you're going to win, you have to be prepared to lose some of the time. Ask a politician a question they don't know much about

and it's likely they'll answer a different question, one they do know about. It's easier for them that way. The problem is you don't have a useful answer to your question. The politician's objective is to be right and save face. And this is the trap decision-makers can fall into. When you answer the wrong-but-familiar question, the result is more of the same. We see a common decision-making problem: lack of relevant data to inform decisions. Are you choosing to answer the right question?

Nobody wants to be wrong, but it's inevitable that the future will not comply exactly with how you imagine it. There are no guarantees for how a strategic intervention will meet expectations. You're going to be wrong some of the time. It's a fact of life. Everything we do involves risk. **Successful choosing will be influenced by how your culture punishes or tolerates being wrong.**

Engage the collective mind

When you need to always be right, you don't leave space for alternative ideas. At Pixar, an entertainment company, managers coax ideas from staff in order to continually stimulate value contribution. Some of these ideas will be wrong. But being wrong is just part of the creative process. When people are attacked for being wrong, they're discouraged from voluntary contribution. Ed Catmull, president of Pixar, and his co-writer Amy Wallace illustrate the point in their book, *Creativity, Inc.*[56] Writing about a 2006 post-screening meeting of an in-progress movie, they quote John Lasseter, chief creative officer of Pixar and Disney, as saying the film had "lost its way." This was just nine months after Pixar merged with Disney and the two different cultures were feeling their way toward integration.

In the meeting at Disney, Pixar producer John Walker wanted to involve the Disney people and hear what they had to say. Instead of fault-finding with the problem movie, he started off with upbeat comments and asked for input. But the Disney employees were reticent to say anything that would be seen as negative. Consequently, they couldn't generate ideas for improvement.

After the meeting, a Disney director confided to Ed Catmull that many in the room had unexpressed reservations. Problems get masked in a culture of fear. There is always a reason why fear exists. You need to first understand that reason before you can address it. Disney Animation's culture was preventing employees from contributing value. By contrast, Pixar has a culture of engagement where mistakes are expected. Pixar's president and producer immediately recognized this unwillingness to speak up as disastrous for a creative company and quickly identified and addressed the problem with Disney Animation's directors.

Involving other people will help you harness the collective intelligence of your organization. Identify and involve influencers.

Default decision habits

How do people within your organization make decisions?

Do default decisions avoid pain at the expense of growth? Industrial psychologist Abraham Maslow thought so. He wrote that in a struggle between safety and growth needs, safety usually wins. Discomfort is something we all have to get used to if we are to grow as individuals. Growth for individuals and organizations is sometimes disorienting. Consider the physical act of walking. For an instant you are off balance between one step and the next. You literally fall forward into the future. You trust you'll keep your balance, and mostly you do. Without accepting a certain amount of risk, you're not just standing still, you're going backwards, because everything around you keeps moving.

It takes courage to discard significant prior investment. This is seen as an admission of being wrong. Courage isn't often talked about in organizational literature, but it's a vital component of leadership. Past effort and sunk costs are no criteria for selection. And there is the stumbling block of decisions made in isolation from realities of customer needs and wants.

Oversimplification is another common problem. When program-of-the-month is the cultural norm, time and effort have to shift toward a more strategic approach. Yet, over time, small steps in the right direction amplify change. **What's important is that these steps are designed to meet strategic goals and are aligned with your organization's values.**

Critical thinking is the antidote to weak arguments. **Does your culture allow for good decision making?**

Consequences

Managers need to make quick decisions. Yet the fear of being wrong limits possibilities. In his book *Being Mortal*, physician and author Atul Gawande writes of regret expressed by many elderly people. Most, at the end of their lives, regret what they didn't do rather than what they did do.

Overall, mistakes have limited downsides. Their benefits far outweigh not risking something different. But consequences of mistakes do vary. Poor judgment pushed General Motors into bankruptcy in 2009. Recklessness brought down Lehman

Brothers. Not listening to changes in the business environment caught Motorola flat-footed, and Kmart failed to invest in its supply chain management. In 2015, news stories broke on Volkswagen's disastrous decision to install software on 11 million of its diesel cars to allow them to pass United States' emissions tests. Once past the test, this software deactivated, causing the cars to release forty times the acceptable levels of NOx. Volkswagen's short-term thinking has done long-term damage, and not only to the company. By some estimates, 58,000 early deaths in the United States are attributable to vehicle exhaust.[57]

Mistakes are part of the learning process. Infants don't just go from gurgling one minute to making eloquent speeches the next. At one end of the spectrum, errors are a normal cost of doing business. At the other end, people will die. How will you measure your risk-versus-reward choices? When results improve, how will you know they are a consequence of your intervention?

What are the consequences of being wrong or right?

Options

You need more than one option to choose from. If consensus is for just one intervention, be sure you look at it from various perspectives. How will your strategic intervention impact different groups? Choosing from an option of one isn't really choosing.

Most hesitation over selection stems from options that are too rigid and inflexible. Predefined options must be subjected to thorough questioning from the strategic framework perspective. Take the case of choosing a consultant. One wants to change your culture. Another has a better product. A third is significantly less expensive. Rather than choose consultants who try to make your culture fit their solutions, choose those who fit solutions to your culture. In this way, **incremental success builds long-term trust** between leaders and consultants.

Be aware of two problems. First, as we've outlined, is the availability heuristic. This rule of thumb operates where you make a quick decision based on only the options in front of you—without necessary time and effort to generate thoughtful alternatives. When this happens, chances are you'll have less than stellar options to choose from. Time crunch can lead to poor choice. Additionally, you may be persuaded by the order in which options are presented. As far as attention goes, it becomes "first come, first served." Not allocating enough time is often a result of lack of perceived value in the expected outcome. Yet the process of choosing is a high-value activity. Like any practice, the more you do, the better you get. Fast decision making is good, but it shouldn't come at the expense of decision quality.

The second problem is presenting too many options for consideration. There's a general belief that more choice is better. As Barry Schwartz points out in his book, *The Paradox of Choice*, we become psychologically overwhelmed by too many choices. However, the previous steps in the framework should have winnowed options to just a few. Our suggestion is to make a final selection from only two or three options.

Let's assume you've had a few wins. You see visible progress. The skeptics are coming around to trusting you. How will you make sure you don't fall in love with your solution? What will keep you looking to improve?

Think value

Continual improvement needs constant focus and resources. We recommend that decisions should be evaluated after the fact. Don't be satisfied with measuring results, because you need to know how you arrived at them. Plan to measure value generated from new behaviors. Be sure to involve representatives from all parties affected by the decision. Ask people to list three items that worked, and three that didn't. Participants must be encouraged to give genuine, constructive feedback. Rather than take an opinion poll with an eye to most common perceptions, look for unique observations. Don't repeat feedback already given. This will keep people thinking rather than merely agreeing with what's been said. What perceptions changed? What did people see that was different? How has your data changed? How can you make better future choices? We'll have more to say about post-choice evaluation in the next chapter.

Consider this...

- Are your choices aligned with the values of your organization?
- What are the criteria for your choices?
- Do you have relevant data?
- How will you use the data you've collected?
- Are you ignoring data?
- How do you currently go about the process of deciding?
- Do managers make it safe for people to be wrong?
- What are the consequences of being wrong?
- What are your expectations of being right?
- Have you allocated enough time to make your choice?
- How does your culture tolerate or encourage dissent?
- Who will you include in the decision-making process?

Chapter 13
Strategic gravity

Genius is the ability to put into effect what is on your mind.
—F. Scott Fitzgerald, Author

Question 10: How will you create alignment?

If you're playing in a band, there are no prizes for finishing your piece of music first. Your objective is to contribute value by harmonizing with the whole. Strategic gravity pulls everyone's effort toward a common objective like a magnetic field attracts objects. First win hearts and minds. Only then will hands and feet follow.

Culture really does eat strategy for breakfast. Strategy dies when ignored, but thrives in a supportive culture. Better communication opens the way for an exchange of ideas. When people are connected to each other, you have the opportunity to benefit from the collective intelligence of the whole. Through connection, communication, and support, you create a space where everyone understands what value is and how they can contribute to it.

Connect

Everybody wants to know. "What's in it for me?" So when you only explain the business case for change, you're not connecting on an emotional level with the interests of employees. Before you communicate, understand what's likely to motivate or demotivate. This goes back to our first question: who is the customer, and what matters to him or her? All of us naturally behave according to our inner convictions. This is why forming relationships of mutual respect and trust are at the heart of self-sustaining systems.

Establishing your strategic gravity field minimizes resistance. Shared beliefs, values, perceptions, and principles shape inside strategy into a self-sustaining force. Alignment isn't just agreement. Nor is it unthinking obedience. Alignment is where people contribute value—in their own ways—within the confines of strategic purpose.

Communicate

If you've considered the previous questions, you now know what you want people to believe, value and do. You maintain this strategic alignment through **constant communication**. The Irish dramatist George Bernard Shaw once wrote that the single biggest problem in communication is the illusion that it has taken place. If people are to become aligned with purpose, they have to know what that purpose is. This is why clear communication is a valuable investment of resources. People need to understand what you say and want.

During World War II, the United States commissioned a series of seven documentary films, *Why We Fight*. We don't know why there were seven films. But seven might be a significant number because many communications experts believe that for a message to stick, it has to be heard at least seven times.

The series title says it all. These documentaries explained the bigger picture and rationale for fighting for a way of life under threat. The purpose was strategic alignment. In order to win, the entire nation had to support the effort. And that support came about through a common understanding of the threat, and belief in the necessary engagement.

At every level of your organization people should be able to:

- Identify their customer(s)
- Know what these customers value
- Know what success looks like
- Understand the "why?"
- Know what's expected of them.

Smart organizations today use a variety of media to explain their purpose to the workforce. Alignment is a result of successful internal communication. You need to talk, talk again, and then talk some more. Effective communication isn't measured by what you say; it's measured by what recipients hear and what they subsequently do.

One point of focus

Creating alignment in a relatively stable culture takes effort over time. But how do you improve performance and extract value where entire companies and contractors come together only briefly to coordinate their effort? The term "adhocracy" was coined by organizational consultant Warren Bennis in his 1968 book *The Temporary Society*. An adhocracy is a flexible and dynamic organization that convenes to do a job and then disbands. Movies are an example, where film crews, writers, actors, technicians, and designers are brought together to perform as teams with a common goal. After the movie is made, the organization separates. People are chosen for their expertise but also for their soft skills, like integrating with others. To work well together, they need direction to comprehend who their customers are and what matters to them, to be aware of changing local conditions, and know the course of the overall project.

We were called in by a large UK company to work on a pilot windfarm project in Northern Ireland. Data showed that project crews spent significant time and resources pulling tractor trailers out of ditches.

These windfarm installations are complex. Logisticians do careful coordination with turbine manufacturers, trucking companies, police, engineers, technicians, land owners, and various contractors. About every two weeks, new teams would arrive, and others, having done their part, would leave. These temporary teams weren't part of a stable culture. **Strategic gravity operates through finding a point of common focus, and then communicating it**.

Here's how we did our work. We met with project management teams and all subcontractors. We started asking our framework of questions. We wanted to identify what success would look like and how we might get there. We looked at the data from previous windfarm installations to see if we could discover missing common control points. We discovered by far their biggest spend was for equipment damage.

Wind turbine blades and towers are massive. Special vehicles are needed to transport such heavy equipment. Steerable wheels on the rear of trailers help them navigate. Despite the fact that crews had widened the narrow country roads, giant tractor trailers were getting stuck. One problem we discovered was that drivers forgot to turn their rear steering off when they got to jobsites. Then when they tried to steer out of a ditch, their rear wheels were facing the wrong way and actually dug vehicles in deeper. This forgetfulness was very expensive. Reminding drivers to turn the rear steering off was simple. But the real solution was for them to drive in the center of the road. Vehicles could pass in established passing locations. Then tractor-trailer wheels didn't go into the ditch in the first place.

Coming up with an idea is one thing. Communicating so it becomes a priority is another, particularly in an adhocracy. "Drive in the center of the road" became part of jobsite induction. It was reinforced by reminder chevrons every 10 meters. It was printed on employees' jobsite badges. Success showed up as behavior change. "Drive in the center of the road" became a **connective conversation** and **a common point of focus.** On this project alone, the company saved millions of pounds. And this behavior change keeps on creating value for future projects.

Tactical trouble

Earlier in this book, we said having no strategy is a strategy. You do have a strategy, even when it's not stated. And if you've stated your strategy, is it what's actually in operation? Are behaviors aligned with the stated strategy? Saying and doing are not the same things.

Peter Drucker identified the absurdity of efficiently doing something that doesn't need doing. When strategy is hidden or unrecognized, all you're left with are tactics, discrete pieces of action. This poses two problems.

First, unaligned tactical success takes you further away from long-term sustainable performance improvement. You may successfully get to the airport in time for a flight, but are you sitting on the right plane? Without a travel strategy, how do you know? You may do some expert marketing, but if the product is defective, you're not creating value; you're causing widespread damage. The tactical objective may be irrelevant, or worse, contrary to the overall purpose of the organization. **When people don't know what to do, they do what they know how to do,** which may be of no value at all.

Author and thinker Edward De Bono coined the term "logic bubble." Decisions make sense within the decision makers' logic bubble. But to those outside of the bubble, these choices may look absurd, meaningless, or just wrong. The logic-bubble focus is a rationale only for tactical success. It's a case of winning battles but losing the war when strategy isn't pulling tactics toward it.

Secondly, when strategy is ignored, the right lessons aren't learned from tactical failure. Failures are a source of valuable knowledge. They tell you to do something differently. When there is no fit between tactics and overall strategy, **these lessons can't be put to use**. This is loss of value. Short-term problem solving must support the overall direction of the organization. Losing shared understanding of what's important takes the pull out of strategic gravity. This is why getting communication right matters.

Don't shoot the messenger

Teenagers, lawyers, and baseball fans have one thing in common. They all speak their own jargon. They're far more likely to listen to a peer who uses their language than to someone else. Your story needs to be told so it makes sense to the listener. A good idea will be rejected or accepted depending on the messenger. What often matters to partisans is not so much policy, but who proposes it. This is why we take pains to identify and include influencers of different groups. They're the ones to deliver motivating messages to their peers.

Speak the language your audience understands. As companies move toward greater effectiveness, discretionary effort becomes the norm. Emotional intelligence is at a premium. As President Theodore Roosevelt said, "The most important single ingredient in the formula of success is the knack of getting along with people." No two people will agree on everything. But people inside organizations must be able to mesh with each other to be effective. This means everyone understands what's important and what's not.

Support

Peter Drucker[58] recounts how Ford came up with a new safety feature in their cars: seatbelts. This was in the late 1940s and early 1950s when automobile safety wasn't part of public consciousness. Ford put seatbelts on the cars without asking for input from customers or explaining the rationale to them. Drivers and passengers hated seatbelts. Ford's sales numbers crashed. People just weren't ready for restraints. In 1965, Ralph Nader's book *Unsafe at Any Speed* brought automobile safety into public consciousness. Subsequently, regulations mandated seatbelts.

Is your culture ready to accept the change you propose? What will your people support? Understanding culture makes clear what is and isn't acceptable.

Strategic support bolsters confidence in people to go beyond the merely adequate. Employees know when they're being supported or hoodwinked, and act accordingly. They know when the organization has their back, and when it doesn't. Are your

- Who will you exclude from your decision-making process?
- Who else could give you input you need?
- What expertise will help you decide?
- What are you willing to give up?
- What are the opportunity costs of making your choice?
- Who and what might you be overlooking?

employees encouraged to communicate, or does your organizational structure limit who can talk to whom? Lack of communication causes informational blind spots. When these grow large, the whole organization is flailing around in the dark.

It's not enough to just give lip service to a collaborative environment. Real support allows people to voice opinions, thoughts, and individual reasoning. Everyone wants to have their input taken seriously. Anything else is hypocrisy. And just about everyone has a sensitive antenna for that. Pretense of support is dangerous. What you'll get is passive agreement, which is just one step above passive aggression. Are people connected or alienated within your organization?

Belonging to a group is a meaningful source of social identity. Support people by including them, and giving each person a chance to weigh in with their views. After hearing ideas, it's the leader's job to arbitrate and explain the reasoning for or against a proposed course of action. What will the most important roles, responsibilities, and results look like? Should incentives or performance management systems be different? What effect would change have?

Make it easy

Attention is a finite resource. When companies aren't getting the results they look for, they tend to add initiatives or programs rather than think about improving the quality of what they're already doing. Adding more initiatives, rules, and plans increases complexity and dilutes attention. Prioritize and simplify strategic focus to align capable effort.

Early in our careers, we discovered that between three and six critical behaviors can prevent 80 percent of accidents in organizations. Since that time, we've expanded this safety observation into a whole range of other areas; ergonomics, customer satisfaction, quality, productivity, and more. We've found the most effective change tool is to **create a productive meme**. First identify what matters, then make it easy to recall. Successful communication is reflected in observable behavior change.

TERRY: Our mantra is this: if you don't get it into their heads, it won't become a habit. Over the years we've come up with hundreds of sets of four to five priorities for different organizations. Even years later, I can recall many of them. For example, about 12 years ago at a plant in Virginia, the acronym we devised was PATH: P=Pace, A=Alignment, T=Tool and H=Housekeeping. This acronym satisfied the question, "Are you on the PATH to safety excellence?" I can remember this over a decade later, but I can't remember the importance of National Safety Council's message from just three years ago. Why? An acronym is better. Stickiness has huge value. Can people recite from memory what's expected of them? They should be able to.

What happened?

Transformational indicators measure contribution to value between behavior and results. Whether your results were successful or not, there are lessons to be learned. Understand what happened. How did you measure value and not just results? An after-action review tells you what happened. You want to see improvement. Have people's behaviors changed so they are aligned with expectations? Waiting for results isn't good enough. What matters is value. And by now you've defined what that looks like.

At a mobile maintenance company, service people work on client equipment at different locations. Our goal was to align people with new knowledge that would change their thinking and thus produce effective behaviors. Our strategic approach started with end-in-mind discussions and a checklist. We wanted people to ask themselves focused questions that would create value-producing awareness. Success would produce a widespread new safety habit.

A six-part checklist was developed.

1. Are we locked out and tagged out? (Is a specific device's energy isolated so nobody can accidentally turn it on?)
2. Do we have the proper personal protective equipment with us?
3. Are we working on the correct piece of equipment?
4. Are there any area hazards?
5. Has anything else changed?
6. What else? What haven't we thought about?

Managers wanted to attach incentives to learning these questions. As we said earlier, be careful with incentivizing behavior. People are motivated to get the reward, and not necessarily the value-producing behavior you want.

We suggested handing out yellow cards printed with the six questions. As the leaders walked around they'd ask, "Hey, do you happen to have that yellow card?" Those who had it on their person got a coupon they could put in for a drawing. And it was a good drawing. There were several winners.

Over the next few months, managers asked the do-you-have-the-yellow-card-on-you question. But they now added a new twist:

before you pull it out, can you repeat two of the questions? Those who knew a couple questions received a coupon for the drawing. Word got around as people started to talk to each other about the six items. Managers kept increasing the number of questions to be answered to get the coupon. About nine months later, they had 300 people on board. Alignment increased. We could see visible progress. Just about anybody you spoke with could name the six questions. Maybe not in the direct order, but that wasn't the goal. On this project, our goal wasn't to directly incentivize behavior, but to incentivize knowledge which would change the way people think. We tested how knowledge spread over time, which created a new beneficial habit. Good managers manage by asking questions.

Success didn't come through new programs; it was **the right framework of questions for employees to ask themselves**. Owners and contractors agreed this was the best project they ever worked on. The ability of the workforce to recite the six important things is an example of a transformational indicator. Knowing what to do is the first step in doing it.

Keeping score

First, the challenge is to improve behavior. Measuring activities in the beginning tells you whether or not you are achieving alignment. Can you see visible progress? Second, you need to know precisely how this happened. Only when you can show how and why you succeeded (or failed) will you start to learn something useful. Are your bets paying off? How have beliefs and values changed? What effect are they having? How do you know you're making headway? Are your priorities right? How are you measuring what just happened?

Robert Kaplan and David Norton have written extensively on the topic of measurement. The pair originated the "balanced scorecard," a strategic planning and management system. According to Harvard Business Review, the balanced scorecard is one of the most influential business ideas of the last 75 years.[59] Decision makers get a "balanced" perspective of static and dynamic information. It's a system for improving organizational performance through measurement.

While the balanced scorecard uses software, it isn't software. It's an approach to strategic management. Similar to the dials in an airplane cockpit, showing everything from oil pressure to air speed, performance measurements can be seen through a dashboard interface. You decide what value contribution to measure: customer satisfaction, emotional temperature of the organization, knowledge, innovation, etc. Using the balanced scorecard, you can track your inputs against your strategic objectives in real time.

A response to a medical test is positive, a reaction is negative. What indicators allow you to determine response or reaction? You don't want surprises. The value of response is that it gives you the opportunity to correct course now, rather than encounter a nasty surprise later.

Transformational indicators tell you about the present and future value. These are new stories and knowledge, topics of conversations, and more functional shared beliefs and behaviors. Do you know exactly why you're seeing improvement or deterioration? Results are a byproduct of behavior. Inside strategy is continual contribution to value through aligned behavior. And keeping that performance-improving process alive is the subject of the next and last chapter.

Consider this...

- Can everyone tell you what's expected of them and why?
- How do you check that your message is understood?
- Is your narrative the right one? Does it include or alienate?
- Who is the best person to effectively deliver your message?
- Have you identified and involved influencers?
- Whose input is needed?
- What can your history of change initiatives tell you?
- What observable behavior change do you see?
- Is your point of focus clear?
- What will people support? Why?
- What will they reject?
- Is your message memorable? Can people recite it?
- What are your top three priorities?
- What are you going to discard?
- How do you know your tactics are aligned with strategy?
- How is your message crafted to be understood by different groups?
- What is your one point of focus?

Part III

Keeping strategy alive

Chapter 14
Living strategy

We are what we repeatedly do. (Misattributed to Aristotle)
—Will Durant, Philosopher[60]

Your organization will either adapt or die depending on its ability to generate sustainable value. What's happening right now is one of two things: it's either evolving toward greater effectiveness or on the path to irrelevancy. For an organization to survive and thrive, people within it must understand and focus on value. Typically, organizational strategy has aimed at besting the competition. But inside strategy turns toward value creation at every level within the organization.

In ancient China, Confucius wrote that leadership is not a means to an end, but an objective in itself. Leadership, like strategy, is an art. Any practice needs constant attention to keep it alive. With practice, you always have opportunity to get better. Benefits grow in the same way that compound interest adds up over time. Living strategy is a way of being, a way of behaving. Most of all, it's a way of asking relevant questions, listening to the answers, and making educated guesses. Inside strategy's focus is not competition among rivals, but creation of value.

Living strategy is a positive habit aimed at **sustainable effectiveness**: finding the right thing to do, and doing it. That "right thing" has to be aligned with your organization's purpose. Inside strategy is active value-creating behavior.

In June of 2006, educator Ken Robinson gave an immensely popular TED talk with the provocative title: "How Schools Kill Creativity." He made a case for creativity being "as important in education as literacy, and we should treat it with the same status." Robinson points out that no one knows what the world will look like in five years. Henry Kissinger wrote, "Analysis depends on interpretation; judgments differ as to what constitutes a fact, even more about its significance."[61] Interpretation is a creative act. But we have a one-sided schooling system. It focuses on left-brain logical thinking at the expense of intuitive right-brain thinking. Strategic thinking needs development on both sides of the brain.

Tactical training

Training focuses attention and teaches specifics. Training is essentially tactical. Tactics are the active components of strategy. Training is more concerned with answering questions than asking them. It works best when it can be immediately applied. But training can quickly become irrelevant when situations change. And change in organizations is constant. There is no question that training is of great value. But it is no substitute for strategic thinking. Training more often than not tells you how, but not why. And training is often a cookie-cutter approach, ignoring the uniqueness and complexity of your organization. Nor is once-in-a-blue-moon training useful. People forget. Moreover, there is a tendency to try to cover every eventuality so trainees are overwhelmed by information that they can't immediately put to use. Training is to tactics what education is to strategy.

Tactics and training are short-term events. One problem with tactics is that they are often abused by being implemented as short-term fixes without regard to strategic direction. Wasted effort bleeds your resources. Strategy and education respond to an unknown, changeable, and uncertain future. Strategy tells you if your training and tactics are relevant.

Strategic education

Learning how to learn is the fundamental task of education. Education equips you for an unknown future. It teaches you to observe, think, learn, and adapt. Asking questions is the essence of strategy. What's your purpose? Is what you're doing still relevant? How does it create value and for whom? Could there be a better way?

Strategy without tactics is just pie-in-the-sky fantasy. Tactics without strategy is directionless activity—busy work. Tactics, strategy, training, and education are all necessary components of a holistic approach to improving performance. Train for tactics: educate for strategy. But make sure your education is not the kind that Ken Robinson says stifles creativity.

Strategy, tactics, education, and training are all part of an integrated whole. But too many organizations aren't paying attention to strategy or education. They train for tactics (skills), but don't educate for strategy (foresight and adaptability).

When employers only look for skills, they're short changing themselves. They are doing what they know how to do rather than doing what needs to be done. Taylorism, as we saw in Chapter 2, still has its effect on industry today. But this mindset is incompatible with twenty-first century realities. Machine-mind encourages unnecessary vigilance and, worse, micromanagement: the best way to stamp out initiative. Yet in an ever more complex future, initiative is exactly what the intelligent company needs.

These ten performance-improving strategic questions never go away. But the answers change as your organization confronts new realities.

Hidden value

In the last chapter, we showed the effectiveness of communicating one point of focus. Yet fresh opportunities will often present themselves as you unearth new information from your data. You may uncover sources of unlooked-for value.

Ralph Waldo Emerson put it well when he wrote, "A foolish consistency is the hobgoblin of little minds." Consistency is often a good thing. Emerson was writing about foolishness as unthinking obedience. As we showed earlier, strategy isn't planning. Nor is it blinkered obedience. Remain alert for unexpected value-generating opportunities. Thomas Jefferson did.

Despite President Jefferson's long-standing personal debt, his plan for the new country was to avert fiscal catastrophe. His number one presidential election promise of 1800 was to erase federal debt. When Napoleon offered to sell 828,000 square miles of the Louisiana Territory for $11.5 million, President Jefferson saw a bargain. He quickly shelled out the greenbacks. Strategy has purpose and general direction. But it needs to be responsive to prevailing conditions and so take advantage of unplanned opportunities.

If you narrow your focus too soon, you can miss new sources of value creation. Not being able to see something in plain sight is called inattentional blindness. This phenomenon isn't a medical condition. All of us have a habit of only seeing what we look for. Not Jefferson. He could see opportunity in the Louisiana

Purchase despite his tight grip on the nation's purse strings. But it's easy to miss the obvious.

How easy?

In an experiment,[62] participants were shown a video of people passing a basketball around. In the video, one team wore black shirts and the other team wore white shirts. The viewers were asked to count how many times the white-shirt team passed the ball. After some thirty seconds, a person in a gorilla suit walked into the picture, beat its chest, and walked out again. Even though viewers looked directly at the gorilla, only half reported seeing it. The other 50 percent's focus was elsewhere. Our ability to focus is a powerful and functional attribute.

This ability is a high-value skill, especially in an increasingly distracting world. It's necessary to shut out information in order to concentrate on what matters. This is good thing. But you also need to recognize there's a cost to focus. Generalists need specialists as specialists need generalists. And this is why organizations require collaboration from individuals with diverse perspectives and interests. The always relevant question is: "What could we be missing?"

This book's intention has been to help you through this best-guessing process.

***

The framework
1. Who are your customers?
2. What's your vision of success?
3. What's your rationale?
4. What's your story?

146

5. What is the scope?
6. What supports or conflicts with your ability to succeed?
7. Where's the relevant data?
8. How will you choose?
9. How will you create strategic alignment?
10. How will you sustain performance improvement?

We've laid the ten questions in a linear form for simplicity. Yet keep in mind, this process is iterative. You may have a vision of success that meets your rationale, only to later discover it would be rejected by your culture; a good idea, but not here, not now. In such a case, you'll need to reevaluate an earlier stage.

Customers

Traditional business strategy defines customers as people who purchase products and services. We defined customers as all people impacted by business processes. Inside your organization, one person's output becomes another person's input. As strategic thinking permeates throughout your organization, everyone should identify his or her customers. Have new ones appeared? Have old customers gone away? What will tomorrow's customers want? What will be of value to them? You need to find out.

Vision

This is the big picture view. What does success look like for you, not just in terms of results, but the value that produces the results? How will you deliver value to your customers? At this point, you're engaging in a creative act of imagination. Overall vision may be designed by those leading the company. Of course, that might be you. Understanding the vision, its ownership, and implementation are the responsibility of all. At the same time, strategic thinking should become a habit for everyone with discretionary effort.

In a 2011 Harvard Business Review article[63], Rosabeth Moss Kanter, a professor at Harvard Business School, writes of zooming in and zooming out as way of benefiting from multiple perspectives. She likens this adaptive vision to the zoom function on a camera. Some people are detail oriented. Others naturally think in more abstract terms. The problem is that two perspectives cause communication problems. People talk past each other.

Dr. Kanter points out the benefits and pitfalls of both views. People who naturally take a narrow view may miss the strategically significant broader context. This is similar to Edward De Bono's logic bubble thinking. A disconnected, limiting view is likely to occur within cultures where information flow is restricted. The problem for the conceptually aware is they can easily miss the devil in the details. The "close in" or "far out" perspectives are both strategically necessary. The negative effect of each can be lessened by refocusing the zoom lens. Quick fixes can mask misdirection. Broad thinking can ignore practicalities. Flexibility and fit are the keys to maintaining a holistic vision.

What small interventions will bring you the biggest effect? What behaviors can you imagine that will bring about performance improvement? Is your vision consistent with beliefs and values? Is your vision easy to understand? Is your vision still fresh and relevant? How will it motivate others to act?

Remember, strategy is a story told in a future tense. What will people be doing? What will you measure? How will people behave? What beliefs and values will they share? How will your organization add value? How will your business unit add more value? How will teams and individuals in them perform better? What low-value activities could you stop doing? Which capabilities are worth further development? Which are not? What else can you do with what you have?

Rationale

Does your vision make sense? Are you asking the right questions? How is your rationale aligned with contribution to customer value? How has your rationale changed? If it did change, what influenced it? If it needs to change, how can you influence other decision makers? Does your rationale still stand up to scrutiny?

Are you clear about the difference between cause and correlation? Could you be falling into the trap of confirmation bias? How will you test it? In response to challenges or new information, are you willing to reevaluate? Can you give a clear and concise rationale?

Being wrong is part of being right. What looks wrong in the short term could turn out to be right in the long run. If you want to get onto a westbound freeway, you may have to head east to find the onramp. Identifying weak spots alerts you to how you can fix them, or rethink your vision. When you don't have a vision, you're likely to copy someone else's. But your culture is unique. Test your rationale early, and test it often. Get input. Keep modifying your rationale so your vision is likely to be realized.

Story

Not having a story means people can't communicate what success looks like. Stories hold the power to inspire action. What's your existing narrative? Is it covert or overt? Which conversations add value, and which don't? Does your story connect people emotionally, or are you just making a business case?

In Chapter 9 we showed how a better story leads to better results. Is your story aligned with existing beliefs and values? Your story needs to be easy to remember and easy to recite. It can be short, simple, and to the point. The same story can be modified for different audiences. But the essence should be strategically the same. What's important is that your story needs to be relevant. It has to be meaningful to those that hear it, and aligned with the objectives of your organization. Tell your story.

Boundaries

In Chapter 10 we asked you to think about the scope. Defining the scope creates a boundary of what you will and won't do, and which items you will address. And, just as important, those items you will not address. Bear in mind, your original idea will probably change as you gather data and test your narrative.

Progress is rarely linear. You may need to reevaluate and correct course. You may come across hidden biases or conditions you can't have accounted for. Then you'll need to go back to earlier stages and reexamine your story, rationale, vision, or customers. Boundaries align effort and expectations.

Culture

Imposing a new system without understand the existing one is asking for trouble. Does your vision fit with your culture? What is your culture telling you? Is your culture going to work with you? How responsive will it be? Will the culture support your proposed intervention or reject it? What existing synergies or antagonisms are present? Understand the political realities of the system you're trying to influence. How will you do that?

We've said much throughout this book about winning hearts and minds. Almost all of us respond emotionally before we do logically. You can get the rationale right and even the story; but if it's a story that misunderstands the emotional temperature of the workforce, you've wasted your time. As we showed earlier, minimizing the perception of change lessens or eliminates resistance. Due diligence reduces surprises.

Data

Many organizations collect data and then fail to use it. Are you using the data you have? What data will help you make small bets? Can you identify lagging, leading, and transformational indicators? What is your data telling you? How will you interpret it? What patterns are you missing? Is there someone else who might draw different conclusions from your data? Why is your interpretation relevant? Are you overwhelmed by the amount of your data? How do you distinguish the signal from the noise? What data are missing? Why is, or isn't, your data trustworthy? Who else might be a source of valuable data? Are you asking the right people the right questions? Are you measuring what's relevant? How do you know?

Has your destination changed as you gather more input from customers? If there has been a change in your initial objective, what happened? Did you discover new constraints or resistances, or new opportunities? What did you learn and how did you learn it?

Choice

As Ken Robinson says: no one can tell what the future will bring in five years' time. But we need to make provisions for likelihoods. Strategy is your best educated guess of how you want the future to unfold. Essentially, strategy works with what you have. Strategy imagines how you can create more value, and then sets about making it happen.

Today, technical tools help us better predict probabilities of future events. But predictions are hardly reliable, as recent elections polls demonstrated. At the time of writing, pollsters have failed miserably to predict recent elections in Israel, United Kingdom, and Poland. And then there is always the Black Swan event: an unlikely occurrence you didn't see coming. Best not bet the farm initially. Are you identifying low-hanging fruit? Are your choices supported by data or opinions? What can you stop doing? What is the most effective choice you can make? Making small bets in the beginning builds confidence. Some choices will be wrong. What will you do when you make a wrong choice? How willing are you to make tradeoffs? What are they? What are your criteria for choosing?

Are you chasing too many priorities? How will you decide what not to do? You may need more resources to achieve your purpose, or you may need fewer. How did you go about making choices in the past? What have you learned?

Alignment

The word strategy comes from the Greek *stratēgia,* the art of generalship. Generals in the army and business leaders are generalists. Command is not the same as business leadership. Yet both commanders and leaders coordinate and rely on expertise of specialists. Alignment comes about when people's beliefs, values, and behaviors are congruent with strategic direction.

People respond to their environment, expectations, peer pressure, cultural norms, and power structures. Change one aspect of the environment and you can change behavior. Richard Thaler and Cass Sunstein in their 2009 book, *Nudge*, write of a simple change to make organ donation a default in Illinois. Previously, a driver had to go through a process of requesting a card and getting two witnesses to sign it. People are free to opt out of this new default system, but this small change makes the desired behavior easy to align with. Leaders today influence change through connection and communication. Acknowledge forward movement because visible progress builds confidence and motivates people to keep going.

Transforming

The good news about indicators is you can measure them. After any intervention, it's wise to measure what happened. You either want to avoid what just happened in the future, or build on your success. Lagging indicators tell you how things were in the past. This is the easiest indicator because the past doesn't change. Unlike the past, the future is uncertain. Leading indicators give you an idea of what the future might bring. At the time of writing, China has just changed its one-child policy to a two-child policy. Aging population and the predominance of men are leading indicators of likely consequences. Early awareness gives you a chance to respond quickly, often with fewer resources. Leading indicators are useful. But they are not perfect predictions of a future state.

Transformational indicators are a special type of leading indicator that measure value and show up as a new and more functional way of thinking and behaving. Transform means to change shape. A transformational indicator measures what and how value is being created and the likelihood of that continuing or growing. We wrote earlier of small changes having big effects, and this is how a transformational indicators work. Take the simple example of learning to read. Achieving this skill opens up a world of knowledge and possibilities that was previously unavailable. Once even a small value-producing behavior spreads through an organizations, it stimulates further advances.

If you've ever ridden a bicycle, you know that to remain stable you have to keep moving. Likewise, your organization is in a constant state of motion. You can achieve dynamic stability through constant focus on winning hearts and minds. Inside strategy is a way of thinking. It expects more of employees than blind obedience and skill acquisition. It gives them the dignity of thinking for themselves. **Strategic thinking operates where change is constant**, and hidden events can rapidly change the landscape. Your organization is a living enterprise. Either rapidly, or over time, it changes shape through constant transformation as it adapts to new challenges.

Inside strategy gives you —and everyone in your organization— a method of managing an unknown future and creating value for your customers, every day.

***

About the authors

Shawn M. Galloway

Shawn is an internationally recognized performance expert and consultant, professional keynote speaker and author of several bestselling books. He has helped hundreds of organizations within every major industry achieve and sustain excellence in leadership, strategy, performance, and culture.

Shawn's strong work ethic came early in life. As a teenager, his father told him, "No one owes you a living. You have to demonstrate new value every day." These words continue to animate Shawn's energetic drive in delivering value to his clients.

Terry L. Mathis

Terry has proven himself a strategic thought leader throughout both his business and consulting careers. He has helped hundreds of clients in over 40 countries to move to the next level in their strategy development, leadership, supervision, employee engagement and safety excellence endeavors. He co-authored three books prior to *Inside Strategy* as well as over one hundred published articles, numerous blogs, podcasts, customized training materials, workshops and keynote speeches.

For more information on how to leverage the expertise of Shawn and Terry, visit www.InsideStrategyBook.com.

REFERENCES

Introduction
[1] *HBR's 10 Must Reads on Strategy*, Harvard Business Review, p.4.
[2] Walter Kiechel III, *Lords of Strategy*, Harvard Business Review Press, 2010, p. 3.

Chapter 1
[3] Joanna Barsh, Marla M. Capozzi, and Jonathan Davidson, "Leadership and innovation," *McKinsey Quarterly*, January 2008, McKinsey & Company.
[4] LTC Goh Teck Seng, "Clausewitz and His Impact on Strategy," *Pointer: Journal of the Singapore Armed Forces*, Vol 25, No 1, (Jan-Mar 1999).
[5] Sir Arthur Conan Doyle, *The Hound of the Baskervilles*, Aladdin Classics June 2000 edition, p. 36.
[6] Charles Caleb Colton, https://en.wikipedia.org/wiki/Charles_Caleb_Colton, accessed June 11, 2015.
[7] Joan Magretta, *Understanding Michael Porter: The Essential Guide to Competition and Strategy*, Harvard Business Review Press, 2012, p. 184.
[8] White paper: http://proactsafety.com/articles/combining-safety-and-quality-a-case-study-from-astrazeneca
[9] https://careers.vanguard.com/vgcareers/why_vgi/story/mission.shtml

Chapter 2
[10] Walt Kelly's 1971 poster for the first Earth Day. https://en.wikipedia.org/wiki/File:Pogo_-_Earth_Day_1971_poster.jpg, accessed December 6, 2015.
[11] Schumpeter, "A palette of plans, Choosing a strategy is a lot more complex for companies than it used to be," *The Economist*, (Print Edition), May 30, 2015, p. 66.
[12] "From headhunters to culture vultures," *The Economist*, (Print Edition), June 13, 2015, p. 65.
[13] Malcolm Gladwell, "Choice, happiness and spaghetti sauce," http://www.ted.com/talks/malcolm_gladwell_on_spaghetti_sauce/transcript?language=en, accessed June 12, 2015.

[14] Philip Evans, BCG, cited by Walter Kiechel III, *The Lords of Strategy*, Harvard Business Review Press, 2010, P6.

[15] Chris Argyris, "Making the Undiscussable and Its Undiscussability Discussable," *Public Administration Review*, Vol. 40, No. 3, May-June 1980, pp. 205-213, published by: Wiley on behalf of the American Society for Public Administration.

[16] John Taylor Gatto, *Weapons of Mass Instruction: A Schoolteacher's Journey through the Dark World of Compulsory Schooling*, [Kindle Locations 1033-1034]. Kindle file.

[17] Richard Dawkins, *The Selfish Gene: 30th Anniversary Edition*, Oxford University Press, 2009, Oxford/New York,
p. 322.

[18] "Triumph." *Encyclopaedia Britannica, Encyclopaedia Britannica Online*. Encyclopaedia Britannica Inc., 2015, accessed December 8, 2015, http://www.britannica.com/topic/triumph-ancient-Roman-honour.

[19] Peter F. Drucker, *The Essential Drucker: Selections from the Management Works of Peter F. Drucker,* Butterworth-Heinemann, 2001, p. 26.

[20] Jerry Jones discusses management style, balance act between owner and GM, Street & Smith's SportsBusiness Daily, March 24, 2014. http://www.sportsbusinessdaily.com/Daily/Issues/2014/03/24/Franchises/Cowboys-Jones.aspx , accessed July 7, 2015.

Chapter 3

[21] Kevin and Jackie Freiberg, *Nuts! Southwest Airlines' Crazy Recipe for Business and Personal Success*, Bard Press, Austin TX, 1996, p. 48.

[22] Ibid., p. 54.

[23] Ibid., p. 121.

[24] "Terrorism Deaths, Injuries, Kidnappings of Private U.S. Citizens, 2011, July 31, 2012,
http://www.state.gov/j/ct/rls/crt/2011/195556.htm, accessed July 18, 2015.

[25] "Heart Disease Facts," http://www.cdc.gov/heartdisease/facts.htm, accessed July 18, 2015.

[26] Abraham Maslow, *Toward a Psychology of Being*, Van Nostrand Reinhold, New York, 1968, p. 152.

Chapter 4

[27] H. R. Colten, B. M. Altevogt, editors, "Sleep Disorders and Sleep Deprivation: An Unmet Public Health Problem," Institute of Medicine (US) Committee on Sleep Medicine and Research, Washington, DC: National Academies Press (US); 2006. Ch. 4, Functional and Economic Impact of Sleep Loss and Sleep-Related Disorders. Available from: http://www.ncbi.nlm.nih.gov/books/NBK19958/.

[28] Shumpeter, "The Enemy Within: Rogue Employees Can Wreak More Damage on a Company than Competitors," *The Economist*, print version, July 25, 2015, p. 53.

[29] "Nicholas William 'Nick' Leeson," *Wikipedia, The Free Encyclopedia*, https://en.wikipedia.org/w/index.php?title=Wikipedia:Citing_Wikipedia&oldid=675836706, accessed on December 8, 2015.

[30] "Burger King Scrambling After Feet-in-Lettuce Photo Hits Web, Adweek, July 18, 2012, http://www.adweek.com/adfreak/burger-king-scrambling-after-feet-lettuce-photo-hits-web-141976, accessed on August 4, 2015.

[31] Eric Schlosser, "Break-In at Y-12: How a handful of pacifists and nuns exposed the vulnerability of America's nuclear-weapons sites," *The New Yorker*, March 19, 2015, p. 46.

[32] *And I Quote*, Revised edition, Ashton Applewhite, William R. Evans III, Andrew Frothingham, St. Martin's Press New York, 2003, p. 237.

Chapter 5

[33] Terry Mathis, "Viewpoint: The Futility of RFPs," Industry Week.com, June 28, 2012, pp. 1-3, http://proactsafety.com/uploads/file/articles/the-futility-of-rfps.pdf, accessed September 1, 2015.

Chapter 6

[34] M. Elisabeth Paté-Cornell, "A Post-mortem Analysis of the Piper Alpha Accident: Technical and Organizational Factors," Department of Industrial Engineering and Engineering Management, Stanford University, October 1991, University of California, Berkeley, pp. 1-80, http://www.bsee.gov/Technology-and-Research/Technology-Assessment-Programs/Reports/100-199/167AB/, accessed September 1, 2015.

[35] "Vision and Values: Integrity," OXY, http://www.oxy.com/SocialResponsibility/overview/Pages/default.aspx, accessed on September 1, 2015.

[36] "Vision of the UTPD: University of Texas at Houston Police Department," http://www.mdanderson.org/utpd/files/utpolicevisionmission-9-5-07.pdf, accessed on September 2, 2015.

Chapter 7

[37] *Annie Hall*, Director: Woody Allen, Producer: Charles H. Joffe, Writers: Woody Allen and Marshall Brickman, Film. USA 1977.

[38] George N. Lewis, "How the U.S. Army Assessed as Successful a Missile Defense That Failed Completely," *Breakthroughs Magazine*, Security Studies Program, Massachusetts Institute of Technology, Spring 2003, Vol. XII, No. 1, pp. 9-13.

[39] Douglas G. Altman, Chapman & Hall/CRC, http://www.ncbi.nlm.nih.gov/pmc/articles/PMC35, accessed September 8, 2015.

Chapter 9

[40] Michael Menard, *A Fish In Your Ear: The New Discipline of Project Portfolio Management*, North Charleston, NC, 2012.

[41] Mike Beraridino, columnist, "Mike Tyson explains one of his most famous quotes," *Sun Sentinel*, November 9, 2012, http://articles.sun-sentinel.com/2012-11-09/sports/sfl-mike-tyson-explains-one-of-his-most-famous-quotes-20121109_1_mike-tyson-undisputed-truth-famous-quotes, accessed September 24, 2015.

[42] "Why your brain has a Jennifer Aniston cell," *New Scientist*, June 22, 2005, Journal reference: *Nature* (vol. 435 p. 1102), https://www.newscientist.com/article/dn7567-why-your-brain-has-a-jennifer-aniston-cell/, accessed September 25, 2015.

[43] Aristotle, *Aristotle in 23 Volumes*, Vol. 21, translated by H. Rackham, Cambridge, MA, Harvard University Press, London, William Heinemann Ltd., 1944.

Chapter 10

[44] Jodi Kantor and David Streitfeld, "Inside Amazon: Wrestling Big Ideas in a Bruising Workplace," *New York Times*, *Business Day*, August 15, 2015, accessed September 28, 2015.

[45] Schumpeter, "Digital Taylorism: A modern version of 'scientific management' threatens to dehumanize the workplace," *The Economist*, September 12, 2015, Print Edition.

[46] Ethan Wolff-Mann, "United Airlines CEO Pledges to Stop Being Awful to Customers and Employees," *Money Magazine*, http://time.com/money/4058048/united-airlines-ceo-oscar-munoz-change/, accessed October 2, 2015.

[47] John P. Kotter and Lorne A. Whitehead, *Buy-In: Saving Your Good Idea from Getting Shot Down*, Harvard Business School Publishing, Boston, MA, 2010, p. 181.

[48] Tonya L. Smith-Jackson, Marc L. Resnick, Kayenda T. Johnson (eds.), *Cultural Ergonomics: Theory, Methods, and Applications*, CRC Press, Boca Raton, FL, Dec 10, 2013, p. 47.

Chapter 11

[49] Ernst & Young Survey, "Sixty-five Percent of College Students Think They Will Become Millionaires," Canada, 2001, cited by R. Salkowitz, *Generation Blend: Managing Across the Technology Age Gap*, John Wiley & Sons, Hoboken, New Jersey, 2008, p. 95.

[50] David Brooks, *The Road to Character*, Random House Publishing Group, April 14, 2015, Kindle Edition, (Kindle Locations 4879-4880).

[51] "Learning Unleashed," *The Economist*, print edition, August 1st 2015, p.22.

[52] A. Banerjee, E. Duflo, N. Goldberg, D. Karlan, R. Osei, W. Parienté, J. Shapiro, B. Thuysbaert, C. Udry, "A Multifaceted Program Causes Lasting Progress for the Very Poor: Evidence from Six Countries, Sciencemag.org, May 15, 2015, Vol. 348, Issue 6236, http://www.econ.yale.edu/~cru2/pdf/Science-2015-TUP.pdf, accessed December 10, 2015.

[53] Dean Karlan, "New Data Reveals Which Approach to Helping the Poor Actually Works," *Reuters*, US Edition, June 17, 2015, http://blogs.reuters.com/great-debate/2015/06/17/new-data-reveals-which-approach-to-helping-the-poor-actually-works/, accessed December 10, 2015.

Chapter 12

[54] Larry Brilliant, "My Wish: Help Me Stop Pandemics," TED.com, 2006, http://www.ted.com/talks/larry_brilliant_wants_to_stop_pandemics?language=en, accessed September 22, 2015.

[55] Thomas E. Ricks, *The Generals: American Military Command from World War II to Today*, Penguin Books, New York, 2012.

[56] John Lasseter, Chief Creative Officer, Pixar and Walt Disney, conversation with Ed Catmull and Amy Wallace, *Creativity, Inc.: Overcoming the Unseen Forces That Stand in the Way of True Inspiration*, Random House, New York, 2014.

[57] "Dirty Secrets: Volkswagen's Falsification of Pollution Tests Opens the Door to a Very Different Car Industry," *The Economist,* September 26, 2015, Print Edition, p. 15.

Chapter 13

[58] Peter F. Drucker, *The Essential Drucker* (*Collins Business Essentials*), Kindle Edition, (2009-10-13), (Kindle Locations 783-786). HarperCollins e-books.

[59] Robert S. Kaplan and David P. Norton, *Alignment: Using the Balanced Scorecard as a Strategic Management System*, Harvard Business School Publishing Corp., USA, 2006.

Chapter 14

[60] Will Durant, (2014-02-06). *The Story of Philosophy* (p. 39), Kindle Edition.

[61] Kissinger, Henry (2011-05-17). *On China*, Penguin Publishing Group, Kindle Edition, p. 363.

[62] Daniel Simons, "But Did You See the Gorilla? The Problem with Inattentional Blindness," Smithsonian.com, http://www.smithsonianmag.com/science-nature/but-did-you-see-the-gorilla-the-problem-with-inattentional-blindness-17339778/?no-ist, accessed October 6, 2015.

[63] Rosabeth Moss Kanter, "Managing Yourself: Zoom In, Zoom Out," *Harvard Business Review*, March 2011, https://hbr.org/2011/03/managing-yourself-zoom-in-zoom-out, accessed October 30, 2015.

Advance praise for Inside Strategy

"This well written guide to strategy execution contains questions that while simple, are amazingly clarifying at focusing us on the path to excellence".
Paul Walsh, President & COO, Ascent Aerospace, LLC

"Through their book *Inside Strategy*, Shawn Galloway and Terry Mathis provide an excellent framework for using strategic thinking to improve performance within any organization. Their work with my former organization helped us to identify the critical few issues, formulate a strategy for change, drive alignment and develop a roadmap for implementation. In this book they lay out a philosophy of continuous improvement that draws on everything from the Greek classics to their experience in the trenches of business."
Stan Golemon, SVP Operations Services, Retired, EnLink Midstream

"Outstanding! Great read for me, especially in the times/ climate we're going through in the energy sector. *Inside Strategy* brings a clear framework to approaching strategy and then determining its effectiveness within your organization. The book is very thought-provoking at making you look at your own organization's effectiveness at value-producing behaviors and how you may or may not be producing them. Chapter 4 Value particularly stood out to me because of my team's constant focus of value creation to the customer and in what form we deliver it (safety or dollar savings). Value creation, internally and externally, is vital to the success of my company's strategy. What is key, especially in this climate and that the book captured precisely, is that value must be lean or it won't last, and that long-term success only comes from continued focus on value. Most importantly, *Inside Strategy* provides a framework that should overlay with your organization's approach/strategy to safety. Though it's not the primary focus of the book, each chapter should be considered as an approach to safety culture and strategy."

Jared Matthias, General Manager—Gulf of Mexico/Sub-Sahara Africa/Mexico, NALCO Champion An Ecolab Company

"Strategy – we can all define it, we think. Galloway and Mathis take a fresh look at this topic and make a compelling case to re-think business strategy in new terms: inside our organizations. Not many companies understand how important our internal strategies are to creating long-lasting business success and deep value. *Inside Strategy* is a thoughtful and thorough piece of work that starts with first principles and leads the reader on a logical and compelling journey. When you are done with the book you will be left with an urgent desire to get to work on developing your own internal business strategies. This book is a worthwhile investment."
Bill MacPherson, Mill Manager, Domtar

"*Inside Strategy* challenges the reader to step outside of the traditional business strategy thinking, and look much deeper in the individual core components that make an organizational strategy successful."
Danial Bravard, Associate Vice President – Risk Management and Safety, Memorial Hermann

"ProAct Safety has been a valuable resource for the reference and implementation of safety culture strategy for over two decades. Inside Strategy artfully takes the impactful ProAct Safety insights of safety culture to the more broad applications of full organizational culture. *Inside Strategy* raises the bar for strategic thinking today and future generations."
Scott Steinford, CEO, Trust Transparency Consulting

"*Inside Strategy* is a must-have for leaders on a mission. When you don't know where to start on your improvement journey, Shawn and Terry offer practical and valuable guidance, almost a road map, for seeing, defining, and setting strategic direction. When you can't quite wrap your arms around an action plan, read this book. *Inside Strategy* takes into consideration where your organization is, where you want it to be, and most importantly, the people that live the culture within it. When you understand, like these experts do, that behavior drives the success you desire, you are more apt to focus on the right things.

Shawn and Terry combine thought provoking questions with accounts of 'been there' that get you to focus on those right things."
Karen Korte Boulanger, Director-Safety, Ameren Illinois

"Most books on safety seem to turn into regurgitated information from all the other books and manuals already in existence. *Inside Strategy* throws all of that out the window. Shawn and Terry bring an approach rarely discussed in a safety aspect when it comes to success - the STRATEGY of how to get there. By building upon the simple three-part concept discussed in the writings, it is almost impossible not to reap the rewards of continued improved safety excellence. This book is a must read at all levels. Outstanding information in an easily understandable format."
Dennis Leonard, Safety Director, Cherne Contracting Company

"Shawn Galloway does it again. He takes complicated principles and makes them simple for all of us. Strategy is so important... but so are tactics. Just like 'executives are important and so are front line leaders'. The penetrating questions he poses in *Inside Strategy* are potent and powerful. I plan to take my multi-national team through this book and answer these questions knowing that it'll make us better, stronger, and more equipped to face the future. (From one U.S. Army veteran to another)... 'Thank you, Shawn for your insight, your passion, and your willingness to help and equip others on their journey towards a Culture of (safety) EXCELLENCE'."
Kirk Bagnal, Director of Global Environment, Health, and Safety Domtar Personal Care

Made in the USA
San Bernardino, CA
21 March 2016